WHAT IF REFORM WINS

WHAT IF REFORM WINS

A Scenario

Peter Chappell

BLOOMSBURY CONTINUUM
LONDON · OXFORD · NEW YORK · NEW DELHI · SYDNEY

BLOOMSBURY CONTINUUM
Bloomsbury Publishing Plc
50 Bedford Square, London, WC1B 3DP, UK
Bloomsbury Publishing Ireland Limited,
29 Earlsfort Terrace, Dublin 2, D02 AY28, Ireland

BLOOMSBURY, BLOOMSBURY CONTINUUM and the
Diana logo are trademarks of Bloomsbury Publishing Plc

First published in Great Britain 2026

Copyright © Peter Chappell, 2026

Peter Chappell has asserted his right under the Copyright,
Designs and Patents Act, 1988, to be identified as Author of this work

For legal purposes the Acknowledgements on p. 227
constitute an extension of this copyright page

All rights reserved. No part of this publication may be: i) reproduced or transmitted in any form, electronic or mechanical, including photocopying, recording or by means of any information storage or retrieval system without prior permission in writing from the publishers; or ii) used or reproduced in any way for the training, development or operation of artificial intelligence (AI) technologies, including generative AI technologies. The rights holders expressly reserve this publication from the text and data mining exception as per Article 4(3) of the Digital Single Market Directive (EU) 2019/790

Bloomsbury Publishing Plc does not have any control over, or responsibility for, any third-party websites referred to or in this book. All internet addresses given in this book were correct at the time of going to press. The author and publisher regret any inconvenience caused if addresses have changed or sites have ceased to exist, but can accept no responsibility for any such changes

A catalogue record for this book is available from the British Library

Library of Congress Cataloging-in-Publication data has been applied for

ISBN: HB: 978-1-3994-3372-3; eBook: 978-1-3994-3374-7

2 4 6 8 10 9 7 5 3 1

Typeset by Lumina Datamatics Ltd
Printed and bound in Great Britain by Clays Ltd, Elcograf S.p.A.

To find out more about our authors and books visit www.bloomsbury.com
and sign up for our newsletters

For product safety related questions contact productsafety@bloomsbury.com

'Our constitution is dangerously vulnerable to capture by the minority who can get hold of a political party which then, for one reason or another, gains a Majority in the House. This state of affairs makes it all too plausible that the worst nightmare of Conservative and Liberal alike – the capture of the executive by a totalitarian clique which would subsequently impose its intellectually disreputable uncertainties at the barrel of a gun – could become a reality.'

William Waldegrave, 1978

Contents

Prologue   viii

1 Election Night   1
2 Victory   35
3 Deportation Nation   65
4 Flood the Zone   105
5 Be Objective   143
6 Up in Smoke   181
7 Limpet   209

Acknowledgements   227

Prologue

Nigel Farage likes to boast Reform has established a 'beachhead' in Parliament. In his telling, the party's eight MPs are the plucky few who, against overwhelming odds, have landed in enemy territory with a mission to capture Westminster. They are in a powerful position to do just that: the Party currently has an army of nearly 300,000 members, an officer class of radical advisors and the support of Britain's most generous political donors. So far, the first assault has succeeded: the Party is ahead in the polls and Farage is the favourite to become Britain's next prime minister. With its high command working on a manifesto and their political rivals in disarray, this book asks: what lies in store for Britain if Reform wins the next election?

Each scenario in this book is based on research and interviews with decision-makers and experts. They include Reform insiders, past and present government ministers, civil servants, constitutional academics, climate sceptics and BBC executives. But each chapter is also an act of imagination intended to illustrate the vulnerability of Britain's unwritten constitution, defunded institutions and fraying political norms to a hostile takeover. Speak to those charged with maintaining Britain's democratic guardrails and they will tell you the moment which worries them most is the next general election. How will a party that wins a democratic election by threatening to 'clear out' Whitehall, abolish the TV licence fee and deport hundreds of thousands of people collide with the establishment? What will those already wielding power do to help or hinder Farage's agenda?

I've invented some characters to represent essential roles in government and elsewhere, such as the Director General of the BBC and the Cabinet Secretary; when I've chosen to describe a real person, it's usually because I think their personalities will be central to a Reform administration. For instance, integral to this scenario are the actions of the men who make up Farage's inner circle of advisors, donors and spin doctors. They're not yet household names but if Reform win the election, they will become as influential as former chief advisor Dominic Cummings was in 2019 or Blair's chief press secretary Alastair Campbell in 1997.

Of course, no one knows for sure what will actually happen: sometimes a pandemic strikes, or a war erupts. A scenario is just one possible future. Here, I've imagined what Farage and his inner circle might do, but no one – not even someone who's been in the public eye for as long as Farage – can be entirely predictable. Some people I spoke to foresee the Party collapsing, Liz Truss-style, within days at the prospect of governing, while others say Farage will echo PM Giorgia Meloni's administrative pragmatism, which has cemented her popularity in Italy. Even the date of the next election is contested: my scenario sees Labour hold it at the latest possible date, while Farage himself claims there'll be one in 2027. Whenever it is, it's more than possible that Reform will not secure a majority: Labour might pull themselves together, or a coalition with the Liberal Democrats may form to block Farage from Downing Street. Even the Tories are far from a write-off. If any of these scenarios become reality, this could be the end of Farage's extraordinary career. Or, it might just delay Reform by another five years.

I've limited myself to Reform's key policies and have not focused on areas such as the NHS and education, where their stated aims are much vaguer. On healthcare, the party has barely announced any new ideas beyond their 2024 manifesto, and on education, there has been little beyond culture war inflected vows to ban the teaching of critical race theory and 'gender ideology' and a promise to make schools 'patriotic'. But since the summer of 2025, when the Party dominated the airwaves through a campaign on immigration, Reform have announced a flurry of policy ideas on the economy, energy and immigration, putting them ahead of other parties before the crucial May 2026 local elections.

I largely wrote this book in the autumn of 2025, so everything about that year and before is a real event. Everything from after February 2026 onwards is informed speculation. Some of the far-right ideas in the book are shocking, but represent ideas which are in the heads of some of the Party's voters and advisors, even though some of them would say Reform is not going far enough.

I'm a journalist and so when I'm speculating on the future, it's usually because I want to know where to look for a story, who to interview next, and how themes today will play out tomorrow. Watching Farage at press events, I began to wonder about not only how Reform would abolish net zero and gut government spending budgets in practice, but also how British culture would react more broadly. If Reform wins in 2029, the result will be the offspring of a stagnant economy, an anti-immigration backlash, a broken housing market, a punishingly high cost of living and a governing party unable to meet those challenges. Despite the drama and comedy of these chapters, a win for the Party has to be seen in that context of declining living standards and a collapse in public trust in politicians.

PROLOGUE

The current Labour government must do everything in its power to create protections for Britain's informal constitution, the BBC and the energy transition while it is still able to do so. It must make the argument for an immigration system which gives those in danger around the world a route to safety. Reform could pose a grave threat to the independence of the national broadcaster, as well as to the rights of protest, both rights successive governments have chipped away at. My investigations have revealed a Britain which is surprisingly vulnerable, a country oblivious to its fragile constitution and almost sleepwalking into democratic disaster. Will it wake up before Farage is in No 10?

Peter Chappell, February 2026

I

Election Night

Thursday, 28 June 2029

4 p.m.

The first people to know that Nigel Farage will be Britain's next prime minister are 10 statisticians in a bunker beneath the BBC. Outside the room, a security guard stands with instructions to bar anyone from entry. The academics inside have all signed non-disclosure agreements.

When an email from a polling station in a Labour marginal drops into their inbox, it is received with stunned disbelief by the recipients. The email contains an exit poll detailing the preferences of only 25,000 voters out of 48.2 million, but the team know what it means, like a seismograph beginning to shake from an earthquake hundreds of miles away.

For the next six hours, results from 140 polling stations begin to flood in. Each ballot is measured against the results from the previous election in 2024 to understand swings of opinion. Psephologists – those who study elections and voting behaviour – are a naturally cautious breed. Exit polls are a prediction, though an accurate one, and they have been wrong before: in 1992, a hung parliament was predicted when in the event the Conservatives held on to their majority. The exit poll commissioned by Britain's major broadcasters and conducted by pollsters Ipsos has in recent years become one of the most trusted and accurate in the world. It is released as soon as the polls close at 10 p.m. and not a moment before – if leaked, it could influence voters, move markets, raise questions about the validity of the election.

'Are you sure? How do we know that? Have we got Wales in yet, what about the Lib Dems?' Professor Colin Rallings asks his team. The team spend the afternoon testing the constituencies using different variables – the number of people in lower-income households, the number of people who own a car – to check for any variation in the pattern this year.

'Perhaps Labour voters will turn up later in the day when they clock off work?' a junior member ventures.

'Not likely. That hasn't been the case for years.'

As the afternoon wears on and Domino's boxes pile up, they begin to prepare to tell the rest of the world what they know.

9.40 p.m.

Professor John Curtice takes the lift up to the windowless newsroom at Broadcasting House. The wild-haired academic is carrying an important folder.

In the meeting room, 15 producers, editors, correspondents, graphics specialists and a few stowaways desperate to hear the results are waiting for him. This year, there are more hangers-on than usual; it has been a tense campaign and the incumbent Labour government has fought hard to close the gap in the polls. There is at least one well-known presenter, however, who refuses to be told the results in advance, preferring to hear them live on air. On hearing the news, there is the uncomfortable mixture of horror and excitement that any journalist feels when they're on a big story. The senior staff exit the room wearing blank expressions, but start firing WhatsApps to those they trust. In 2015,

ELECTION NIGHT

Andrew Neil told his guest on the BBC's general election night coverage show, former Lib Dem leader Paddy Ashdown, simply: 'You will get a shock.'

Meanwhile, at Labour HQ, advisors are clustered in groups, running through three scenarios: Labour majority; Labour largest party, meaning a hung parliament; Reform UK largest party. Hopeful, realistic, nightmare ... A scenario where Reform secure a majority isn't countenanced.[1]

At his count in the leisure centre where his son first learned to swim, a Labour minister rings his advisor to ask how the mood is south of the river.

'The polls have said it's too close to call, but we're thinking a slim win. Tactical voting and high turnout will get us over the line. Feeling here is that we'll just about do it,' he replies.

9.55 p.m.

The BBC's coverage goes live. Scenes from the election flash across the screen: the prime minister at a polling station with their family, Lib Dem Leader Ed Davey shaking hands with Paddington Bear, Kemi Badenoch looking angry at a vape shop. There's a drone shot of the Palace of Westminster, then the BBC's Laura Kuenssberg and Clive Myrie appear outside a virtual Downing Street. A clock ticks down the seconds until the exit poll.

10 p.m.

There are a few audible gasps from the dozens of Labour staffers gathered around the TV screens, but apart from

---

[1] This was the case in 2015 when the polls predicted it was so unlikely that the Tories would get a majority that Labour did not prepare an initial response for Harriet Harman to read on a tour of broadcast studios.

that, silence. All the air has vacated the room at Labour HQ. The banner across the screen reads: 'Exit poll predicts Reform largest party'.

10.01 p.m.

'If you are part of Labour tonight and you are absorbing these numbers for the first time,' Laura Kuenssberg intones, 'then clearly, they are very bleak and could point to a long way back for the Party if that's how things stack up as results come in tonight. It will have left many in the Party utterly shell-shocked. Labour has gone from winning a landslide with 405 seats in 2024 to just 144 today. Farage only needs this poll to be underpredicting his performance by a couple of percentage points and he has an outright majority in the House of Commons.'

10.02 p.m.

Labour's chief of staff at HQ calls the prime minister, who is watching with their partner from the flat at No 11 Downing Street. The command is to deny the poll and stall any speculation on the results.

10.03 p.m.

'With all the confidence I can give you, it's wrong,' the deputy prime minister tells Clive Myrie and Laura Kuenssberg on the BBC.
'We've led a positive campaign, unlike our opponents. I'm proud of our manifesto. I've been knocking on doors

all day and positive signs have been coming in from those I've spoken to and from candidates. There's a huge amount of disbelief and scepticism being directed at this poll internally, I can tell you that, Clive'.

10.04 p.m.

In Southwark, however, four minutes after the exit poll the alarm turns to panic: this is real. Nobody's watching the BBC anymore, everyone's on WhatsApp or a call, trying desperately to work out how they could have got it wrong. The prime minister's partner is wondering how they're going to move all their possessions out of Downing Street in under 48 hours. Sometimes, as in 1992, there are talks between opposite numbers to arrange for the easy transition to a new occupant in No 10.

Not this time.

10.15 p.m.

A tweet appears on screen from Lewis Goodall, podcast presenter and LBC host: 'Extraordinary rumours are circulating in Leeds West and Pudsey. Labour people are refusing to chat but it is being claimed by people in the count that Rachel Reeves might lose her seat. Reform think they've just about done it.'

'Do you think she's going to go?' journalist Chris Mason asks Laura Kyrke-Smith, a Labour MP in Aylesbury who is sitting on the BBC's panel.

At first, she dismisses the question out of hand. 'This exit poll and this sort of chatter about Rachel is hyperbole heaped on speculation heaped on hypothesis. But I should say that if she does go then she should have a long hard think on how she caused what we are seeing tonight.'

10.40 p.m.

The first results come in from Blyth and Sunderland. Reform has won both seats by an enormous majority.

'Swings of this kind are backing up the exit poll, which has come under some criticism from Labour and other parties. In fact, if anything, Reform are exceeding expectations in these results. What we are seeing is confirming our predictions nicely,' says Professor John Curtice, author of the exit poll. 'It seems like the Birkenhead Bounce, where polls after Labour's mass rally on Merseyside shifted to the prime minister at the last minute, are not making themselves felt so far,' he adds.

BBC News presenter Adam Fleming is at the interactive board, analysing the latest result from Houghton and Sunderland South, where the transport secretary Bridget Phillipson has been re-elected. But not as comfortably as Labour figures would have hoped.

'What we're seeing is a rise for Reform UK in an area of the country that is historically staunchly pro-Labour and more left-wing than the rest of Britain. In 2024, she enjoyed a majority of over 7,000 and that's been slashed to just 150 today. Phillipson was a Starmer loyalist until his downfall and there were many reports when she ran for the deputy leadership in 2025 that she did so because of a request from Downing Street to see off Lucy Powell. It's only one result, Clive, and one swallow does not make a summer, but we'll be watching for this effect as more and more results come in.'

10.50 p.m.

Myrie and Kuenssberg discuss the decimation of the Conservative Party.

'The Conservatives once liked to boast they were the most successful political party in the world. That claim has felt shaky for years, and based on the exit poll, voters have outright rejected it, Clive. I'm already receiving WhatsApps here from angry Conservatives who blame leader Kemi Badenoch for unofficial overtures to Reform, which at this point in the night seems to have done little to prevent their obsolescence and given them nothing to distinguish themselves from with voters on the doorstep. Many on the campaign trail told me: Why vote Conservative when you could end up with Labour? The leaked letter in which Badenoch was seen to offer a deal with Farage must have hurt them. Many of their traditional voters in places like Cheltenham or Surrey Heath have fled to the Lib Dems and the red wall — remember that? — is being painted turquoise. Just look at this result in Sunderland. Sure, the Tories were never expecting to do well here, but their candidate actually lost their deposit. That's a historically bad result in that part of the world for them, and it shows how Farage is doing an astonishing job of consolidating the right-wing voting bloc.'

11 p.m.

There's a collective groan at Labour HQ as they watch footage of Reform's Shadow Work and Pensions Minister Lee Anderson driving into the car park outside his count in a 1960s turquoise three-wheeled Invacar — or invalid carriage, a car distributed by the NHS for decades after the Second World War — purchased to campaign for cuts to the

Motability Scheme. The stunt secured huge coverage and Anderson's star had risen over the past six weeks.

11.03 p.m.

Anderson enters the count in Ashfield armed with a T-shirt cannon launcher, firing tops with 'Family. Community. Country' written on them at the assembled activists, most of whom are chanting 'send them back'. The BBC reporter tells viewers that Anderson, a former miner and Labour councillor, is set to comfortably win the seat. The camera loses him for a moment, before his shock of white hair bobs above the sea of supporters, as polyester bullets go flying across the hall. The returning officer, the official charged with overseeing the election in their constituency, mounts the stage to plead with him to stop.

'Would the Reform candidate please stand quietly and refrain from firing T-shirts. Please could he obey the guidelines as set out in the candidate handbook,' the official begs.

'Calm down, love,' Anderson tells her, beaming at his team, who together perform an exaggerated snigger. The launcher thumps another T-shirt across the tables piled with votes. For a time before the election, Reform worried that his record of bullying and harassment would damage the Party's appeal with voters. In 2023, Lee Anderson was punished by Parliament's watchdog on bullying and harassment for verbally abusing a member of staff when they asked to see his pass on entering the Houses of Parliament – 'Fuck off, everyone opens the door to me, you are the only one,' he had said. Was he too hard to handle? But Anderson had a knack for a blunt soundbite and eye-catching stunt so useful in an election campaign that they withheld their scepticism, for now.

A hush goes around and Anderson's advisors fall into an expectant silence for the results. To those watching the pantomime at home, it's becoming clear that Britain is heading in a very different direction.

Midnight

A young LSE graduate fresh from three years in the charity sector and representing Labour wears a rictus grin as she is trounced in Derby; the Rt Hon Sir Roger Gale, who has served the constituents of North Thanet since Margaret Thatcher's day, is humiliated in Kent. Being 85, he had wanted to retire at the election, but Badenoch made him stand in a desperate attempt to hold back Farage. Lined up against the 19-year-old Reform candidate on the squat stage, Gale takes the news with a sanguine air. The winner runs off into a group of supporters holding foam fingers aloft, 'Let's Save Britain' printed across them.

Friday, 29 June 2029, 12.05 a.m.

'Britain takes a leap into the dark,' runs *The Times*' late edition headline. 'As Britain gets Reform government … we're "COCK-A-HOOP!"' screams the *Daily Mail*, quoting Farage's phrasing from a video posted to social media a minute after the exit poll. 'Farage Barrage,' says the *Sun*, who had switched their allegiance from Labour to Reform a year before. 'Let's hope there's plenty of butter at Labour HQ, because the party is toast!' the inside editorial ran. The *FT* led with uncertainty in the markets, but investors' eyes are drawn to a down-page headline predicting a 'Trump-style stocks surge' if Reform Shadow Chancellor Richard Tice's deregulation policies become reality. The *Guardian* publishes an edition with black borders in mourning for Britain as the newspaper's subscriptions manager posts to LinkedIn about a record response to its well-timed donations plea.

1.30 a.m.

'From now until 4 a.m. is the key period for results,' the BBC's Jeremy Vine tells viewers. He stands astride a constantly changing electoral map of the UK, where minute by minute tiles are turning turquoise.

'In the British electoral system, when a party hits 25 to 28 per cent of the vote, pollsters have shown that they start racking up seats very quickly,' he adds. 'The trouble Reform had at the last election was that they couldn't quite get there: the Party's vote was very "inefficient", meaning they got a lot of votes, but couldn't turn them into seats.[2] This time, everything is different. Farage is being aided by the Greens and Lib Dems eating away the Labour vote and the shocking collapse of the Tories. In Scotland, the SNP have won back many of their old seats from Labour. Tactical voting has been a massive part of the picture, but according to this exit poll it has been far more successful on the right than the left. Many voters have looked at the Labour rally in the polls and thought they'd give them a chance, but just not enough to bring back all those they lost to the Greens.

'Tonight, we are going to be keeping a very close eye on the East Midlands. We're watching Nuneaton: a very important part of any election battleground are these Middle England places which are weighing up whether they can see Farage in Downing Street. Mansfield and Ipswich are other examples. We're also keeping tabs on places like Reading West and Kettering, which sound a little bit prosperous. People might

---

[2] This was the opposite of Labour in 2024, which won a lot of seats on a low vote share.

be surprised to see areas of the country which they think are doing comparatively well turn out for Reform tonight.

'There was a lot of froth about a potential deal between Reform and the Tories, wasn't there, Clive?' Vine continues, turning to his colleague. 'If they had done a deal and it had worked, we could have seen a huge Reform majority tonight. If that had happened, there would have been hundreds of seats where there was only one right party and three or four left-wing parties. But it eventually came to nothing as the two parties couldn't agree on where they would stand down for each other. However, similar to Labour and the Lib Dems in 2024, locally there were some informal agreements, which might have kept the Tories from a total wipe-out: despite the lack of an official pact, there were reports of deals struck where the Tories didn't fight in certain areas, in exchange for Reform pulling back resources in what is left of the Conservative heartlands. While this will keep the Tories on life support after the election, the consolidation of Britain's right-wing bloc is helping drive Reform to an outright majority.'

There is a huge swing to Reform in Swindon North, which has been high on their target list. Former Chancellor Rachel Reeves is steely-faced as she is beaten by 20 votes in Leeds, after three recounts, by a former blackjack dealer from Croydon. Pat McFadden in Wolverhampton South East hangs on, but only by a whisker. A photograph of Wes Streeting with his hands raised in exasperation as he is beaten by Zarah Sultana in Ilford earns its place at the top of the *Guardian*'s live blog. Such is the wild whooping at the fall of one Labour minister that the reading of the results at both counts has to be abandoned and restarted when the audience calms down. Sir Keir Starmer, who almost drifted into obscurity after stepping down, hung on comfortably in Holborn and St Pancras, but with a significantly reduced majority. Like Theresa May and Rishi

Sunak before him, Starmer chose to stay on in Parliament: he served on the Justice Select Committee and campaigned in favour of the ECHR. He had taken on a role at the Blavatnik School of Government in Oxford, where he designed a course on Civil Service reform. This being one of the safest Labour seats, there were few journalists at the count, but Starmer sought out who he could find and ended up cornering a trainee BBC Radio 4 reporter, who broadcast the interview live for listeners: 'People, whatever they tell the pollsters, when they are in the ballot box will be thinking about the economy and about immigration, and Labour has not managed to land the message that we can be trusted on those two issues. And that is the fault of some in our party and the reckless coup. We were making so much progress: yes, it was slow and steady, but we would have got there. This is their night; the blame has to lie with them. Reform cannot be trusted with those issues, recent experience has proven that. But there are enough people who have been taken in by that myth today to vote in many Reform candidates.' The reporter's eyes widened. He had rarely heard Starmer talk with such conviction before. Suddenly he was fluent, unstilted. Almost charismatic. Why had he not shown this much fire when he was PM?

'The awful thing is that it will be those people who will be hardest hit by all the awful, rapacious things that Reform are about to unleash on this country,' Starmer continued.

Victoria Starmer, having tracked down her wayward husband, collected him with an apology and took him home.

Meanwhile, Reform take seats from Labour and Conservatives alike. Former MP for Surrey Heath and editor of The *Spectator* Michael Gove is on the BBC: 'Before our eyes we are seeing a grand old first-rate ship of the line being tugged out for scrap. The party of Disraeli and Churchill has likely fought its last battle. Many will mourn her passing.' Despite the carnage of the night, Labour HQ is delighted by the state of the Tories. Tribal to the last, many in the Party, including Starmer's former chief of staff Morgan McSweeney, consider Reform to be bad, but the Tories as 'scum'.[3] The dissolution of the Conservatives is not the only historic shift making itself evident. The night is seeing a new type of MP born. Starmer's lawyers, journalists and doctors are trounced by veterans, self-employed accountants, professional landlords, driving instructors, pub landlords, farmers and call-centre managers, as well as financiers and landowners. In other ways, it feels like Parliament is returning to the twentieth century: in 2024, 40 per cent of seats in the House of Commons were occupied by women MPs. In this scenario, if the exit poll is correct, it will fall to 22 per cent.

In 2025, one of Reform's outriders, Gawain Towler, had put out a call that the Party were looking to recruit candidates who weren't 'the shiny-suited careerists who infest Westminster like cockroaches in a greasy spoon'. They wanted 'hardy souls' ready to 'charge the establishment's machine guns'. He said candidates had to understand they would be 'lobby fodder', their 'ambitions subordinated to the greater war'. Few Reform MPs celebrating at their counts will be given a ministerial role and Farage will need his backbenchers to remember that they are mere foot soldiers in his revolution.

But some MPs are fated to be generals. In Fareham and Waterlooville, Suella Braverman, Reform's shadow education secretary, is re-elected; Ellie Reynolds wins in Barrow-in-Furness, beating the Labour candidate Michelle Scrogham by thousands of voters. 'When Reynolds resigned from the government's inquiry into grooming gangs and held a joint press conference with Nigel Farage in October

---

[3] According to a Labour source.

2025, it was a sign of things to come, and grew into a rallying cry for Reform. She's now tipped as the nation's next social services minister,' says Channel 4's political editor Gary Gibbon. Matt Goodwin, likely the next minister for higher education, is narrowly elected after a close contest with a local Green candidate, a result Reform particularly savours following their loss to Zack Polanski's party at the Gorton and Denton byelection in February 2026. Rishi Sunak is beaten in Richmond and Northallerton, and Sunak's wife Akshata Murty's outraged reaction on behalf of her husband typifies the scale of the Conservative loss. Sunak's humiliation is deemed the night's Portillo moment. Danny Kruger, an old Etonian who worked in Downing Street with Boris Johnson before defecting to Reform in September 2025, justifies his betrayal by winning Wiltshire East. Many speculate that he will be made foreign secretary. One setback for Reform was the surprise loss of Zia Yusuf, the party's shadow home secretary, who was beaten following a recount by the Labour candidate. 'He can be sure of a top role in government, regardless', Gibbon says. Robert Jenrick, who had served as Reform's shadow chancellor until 2028, wins in Newark. That year, Farage's men had discovered a plot by Jenrick to oust him as leader but had hushed it up in a bid to maintain party unity before the election. The former Conservative minister had been moved to health to avoid embarrassment.

In 2025, Dominic Cummings described Reform as being made up of 'Nigel and an iPhone'. 'But they can't win an overall general election and have a plan for government and have a serious team able to take over in Downing Street and govern and control Whitehall with one man and an iPhone.' These newly minted MPs are the men and women who will become Farage's front bench, his vanguard who will stage Reform's hostile takeover.

3 a.m.

Just before the exit poll was announced, for an unnerving second Reform's director of communications, Dan Jukes, had felt a terrible sinking feeling and he'd seen it in Farage's face too. But a second later, he was shaking with joy. As Big Ben struck 10 and the number flashed on the screen, Farage leapt up and hugged him, knocking half-empty glasses of red wine on to the carpet of his Chelsea apartment. The flat's location and Farage's tipple of choice were something the team preferred to keep quiet: while he liked to appear a man of the people, he hardly lived like one. One former Reform insider has even said he is so known for his love of wine in the United States, some of Trump's people call him 'Mr Red Lips'.[4]

But he wasn't prime minister until he had secured Clacton. After the exit poll, Farage was driven straight to the count, where he bounded on to the stage, barging in front of the other candidates, putting on a show of his Union Jack socks for the hive of paparazzi swarming at his feet. This was the man that after a speech a week earlier, the *Economist*'s political editor had said: 'Listening to Mr Farage yesterday, it was no longer impossible to imagine him in Downing Street.' Watching it all on her phone at her count in North West Essex is the Conservative leader Kemi Badenoch, who is waiting for a call from Farage to begin talks on a coalition government. But none arrives. Later, a Reform advisor texts to say they are holding out for a majority.

3.35 a.m.

Among the Clacton candidates is the comedian Chabuddy G (real name Asim Chaudhry) from the BBC mockumentary

---

[4] Far from being the heavy pint drinker of his public reputation, Farage prefers a gin and tonic in private, or a glass of wine, according to a Reform source.

show *People Just Do Nothing*, entered under his adopted name 'Nigel Garage'. He is wearing a tracksuit and a gold necklace which says 'ReformFM' and is Farage's main opposition for the Clacton seat after shooting up the polls following a series of pro-migrant music videos filmed on the pier. Even Dan Jukes could admit it would be a bit funny if Farage was stopped from being PM by Chabuddy G.

Jukes stares at the rogues' gallery of candidates, arranged behind the returning officer.

'How are we feeling?' he asks Peter Harris, Farage's election agent.

'It would have been quicker to weigh them,' Harris mutters, staring at the stacks of slips.

'The total number of votes was 45,032,' says the returning officer. 'The number of ballot papers rejected was seven. The number of votes recorded for each candidate at the said election is as follows.'

'Garage, Nigel Paul, ReformFM: 9,549 votes.'

'Farage, Nigel Paul, Reform UK: 30,393 votes.'

Jukes grins as he spots the press team's self-conscious seriousness of moments before turning to hooligan ecstasy, forcing the returning officer to demand silence. Ed Sumner, rotund and pale, with a finely sculpted ginger beard; John Gill, dark eyes with a combover, and boyish Jack Anderton, a teetotaller, always carrying a camera. They were a gang, formed over nights in the Westminster Arms and invites from Farage to the private dining room at Boisdale's, a Scottish restaurant and jazz bar tucked in behind London Victoria and frequented by Reform types with expense accounts. The Canary Wharf outshoot was where Farage had held his 60th in 2024. But the biggest nights would often start at a free bar event in Westminster, then on to a pub until closing time before going back to someone's house in west London until the early hours.

East Wiltshire's Danny Kruger likened the Party's insiders to a 'pirate ship' in October 2025. It's 'led by a buccaneering, charismatic captain, an ill-disciplined crew – but a powerful ship with a dangerous broadside, a terror to its rivals,' he declared. Since that glorious summer of 2025, when they had ripped into the hull of every major party with a series of immigration stunts and press conferences, the Party had firmly moved into the mainstream and was the real Opposition in the eyes of the government. This left little room for renegades, and any privateers not with them were quietly shown the plank. They had to professionalise, Farage said, and tasked Reform UK head of policy Zia Yusuf to bring data into their operations.

Before the election, they bombarded the government with Freedom of Information (FOI) requests. Screens went up in the office showing the latest stats on immigration, A&E admissions, and arrests. Whereas in 2022 the boys worked from a tiny space in Victoria and bickered about chairs, now they had an HR manager and a conference room looking over Westminster in Millbank Tower. There were corner offices for Farage and Yusuf, paid for by a flood of donations. In December 2025, Reform announced it had been donated £9 million by cryptocurrency investor Christopher Harborne, the largest sum ever given to a political party by a living person. The old room for smoking when they couldn't be bothered to go downstairs had been converted into a podcast studio, lunches could be no longer than 90 minutes and scheming by the coffee machine was just as common as over a Guinness or four at the Marquis of Granby around the corner.

But Downing Street is a prize far greater than free espresso and a party laptop. First the exit poll, and now watching Farage's re-election speech: they realise this is the real deal.

3.37 a.m.

While Farage and his pirate crew celebrate, at Labour HQ the post-mortem has already commenced. The victory speech at Battersea Power Station had been canned and advisors picked to stand on Downing Street to clap had been stood down.

After pursuing a policy of eye-watering tax rises and despised benefits reform, Starmer had been ousted a couple of years previously in a coup. The new prime minister had immediately taken the hard decision to raise income tax, which had allowed the new government to raise investment in the NHS and to throw some red meat to the left of the Party by scrapping welfare reforms. On immigration, they attempted to strike a middle ground between the Greens, who were in favour of open borders, on the left, and Reform's policy of mass deportations on the right. But the PM found it an almost impossible task holding their party together on the issue. As they told MPs at a Downing Street reception: 'If we hold our noses and do what needs to be done on the border today, we will build a New Jerusalem tomorrow.' While this wasn't a radical change from the Starmer years on policy terms, with the change of leadership and sharper communications strategy, Labour had felt it was in with a fighting chance. Things were seeming to improve so much that Denise Coates, head of the online gambling firm Bet365, had even come out in an interview just before the election saying someone had taken a bet on the prime minister to remain in office for £500,000, one of the largest wagers of its kind in British history.[5]

4.32 a.m.

A clutch of Labour special advisors huddle around one of the TVs, each clutching a warm glass of prosecco. They

---

[5] In the 1992 election, one punter was so confident that Neil Kinnock would be the next PM that he put a £20,000 bet on the outcome. He didn't win.

might as well not waste it, someone had said. Labour's chief of staff, who had put together the campaign, hadn't been seen in hours. In the weeks before the election, most of their colleagues had been sent around the country to knock on doors. If they landed in an area where it was obvious Reform were way ahead, the teams had clocked off early and headed to the pub. But in many areas, volunteers and staffers had desperately knocked on doors to get the vote out to stop Farage right up until the polling stations closed at 10 p.m. Places which were formerly safe seats had become battlegrounds, with Labour looking as if they might lose swathes of Greater London. At 4.32 a.m., everyone still awake is dead on their feet.

At the start of the campaign, there had been little enthusiasm for the governing party, which lay far behind in the polls. But the Labour strategists' prediction had come true: as people woke up to the threat of Farage, there had been an influx of energy and determination, encouraged by the fact that, in the words of the Party's chief of staff, the country's 'vital signs' were in their favour. It's common before elections for voting blocs to become more efficient. The media became fascinated by the new Labour leader's 'fightback narrative' and the momentum of the election campaign was powered by a supposed Labour recovery. In 2024, Rishi Sunak attempted to channel the same energy, but it never materialised. This time felt different.

Inflation was under control, growth ticking up and NHS waiting times were down. There was also more than enough ammunition to fire at their opponents. They pointed to Reform's ineptitude in local councils as evidence for their inability to run public services. The leadership's critics said they had failed to address the root causes of inequality and had extended the managerialism under Starmer. It was true that Labour had not had a good start in government, but all administrations front-loaded bad things. Once they started to deliver more policies that impacted people's lives, voters would move back to the Party in 2029. Right?

As they watch, more and more of their colleagues begin to lose their seats, and they start to question how it all went wrong.

In 2029, a general mood of dejection and distrust pervaded the country, leading to unexpected issues like the health of the high street becoming salient. Reform had enjoyed success with a 'Back British Barbers' campaign to boycott Turkish shops and their policy of council-regulated quotas on the number of vape shops was popular. The visible degradation of the public realm outside London spoke to a greater malaise. The drinks industry warned that pubs were closing at a faster rate than ever, while the Confederation of British Industry (CBI) raised concerns that people were turning more and more to bargain deals at supermarkets to make ends meet. Queues at food banks were at their longest on record. London was still an international city, but beyond it there was an ineffable sense that the social fabric had weakened, perhaps permanently. The National Police Chiefs' Council (NPCC) warned of an unsettling spike in violent crime, although other commentators noted incidents of crime in general was still on a downward trajectory. Images of crumbling parish churches in empty villages circulated social media, as did right-wing accounts sharing videos from life in what they called 'the Yookay': a carefully edited, AI-slop hellscape of Deliveroo drivers, Islamic gangsters, drill videos and chicken shops. The term, coined on X, had become so common that Kemi Badenoch had used it in a speech at a rally. Reform's 'alarm clock Britain' slogan, which spoke to voters who felt they were getting up early and working hard while others benefited, had caught the public imagination, given how the country had changed: more people worked early mornings and late evenings in insecure work, voters were increasingly self-employed and freelancing, hustling from one job to the next.⁶ Meanwhile, foreign commentators looked on in horrified fascination at how Britain appeared to be returning to the days of the shop-soiled 1970s.

The advisors can barely watch the horror show in Clacton. But they can't stop the inevitable: Farage exits the count and bins his rosette. He hops into the waiting car. Next stop? GB News.

6 a.m.

Wedged just across the canal from Paddington station, GB News has a bunker mentality. It sees none of the light from dawn on the first day of the new political era. The air conditioning gives you a sore throat. Its three top-of-the-range sets are spread across a floor the size of a football pitch, with a small green room for hosts at the back so they do not mix with guests.

Labour advisors back in London watch it all live, reeling from the sight of the prime minister conceding the election just a few minutes before. 'Half the lobby's there!' says one, between taking calls from distraught former MPs.

Farage, watching the broadcast from HQ, steps out on to the pavement in front of the studio. Those watching are silent as Farage is told live on camera that he has reached the magic number: 326 seats in the House of Commons. The exit poll was wrong, Reform has won an outright majority. Once all the votes have been counted, the final result will be: Reform on 335 seats, a majority of 20; Labour on 124 seats; Liberal Democrats on 79, the SNP on 45, the Tories on 23, the Greens on 11, Plaid on six and independents on 13.

---

⁶In his speech announcing he was joining Reform in January 2026, Robert Jenrick said he was on the side of workers who are 'out the door at 6, 7 a.m. Grafting all week but finding nothing left over for something nice with their kids on the weekend. Their bills and taxes surging. Their money taken to fund hotels for those illegally in our country.'

WHAT IF REFORM WINS

When the Speaker and their deputies are taken into account, as well as the abstentionist Sinn Fein MPs, Reform's working majority stands at 27.

A 12-piece band, massed at the broadcaster's entrance and dressed in red Grenadier Guard jackets, strikes up, playing 'Rule, Britannia!' as Britain's next prime minister arrives through the double doors. He doesn't stride; the 65-year-old has the walk of an older man, stiff and slow. From around the corner, Andrea Jenkyns, the shadow energy secretary, emerges in a sequined dress with a microphone and a cameraman, and starts singing, using her phone for the lyrics:

> When Britain first, at heaven's command
> Arose from out the turquoise main
> Arose, arose from out the turquoise main
> This was the charter, the charter of the land
> And guardian angels sang this strain.

The anthem goes on for longer than the singer or audience expected and eventually, GB News boss Angelos Frangopoulos orders the sound man to gently fade her down. Meanwhile, GB News journalists, even the grads who have been in the job five minutes, line the foyer to clap the great man in, his team following on behind, hugging and fist bumping their friends in editorial, while others are furiously banging on their desks. They have all changed their ties to turquoise blue. Farage had once been the station's big signing in 2021, right at the moment when things had looked most difficult for the fledgling channel, and had bagged them two gongs at the Television and Radio Industries Club awards. This was something of a homecoming. The amount of money that poured in from GB News to Reform MPs for their various appearances on its panels and shows would, even in 2025, have made it one of Reform's largest donors if the funds were classed as political donations. In the years since, the relationship has grown ever more symbiotic. Now party and broadcaster have become indistinguishable.

6.02 a.m.

The news that Farage has won the UK general election is making waves around the world. A post from Truth Social suddenly flashes up on the screen next to Myrie and Kuenssberg: 'CONGRATULATIONS to the People of GREAT BRITAIN! I am watching England's next Prime Minister Nigel Farage WIN BIG tonight. He is a HUGE supporter of MAGA and @POTUS JD Vance. There is much to be done to benefit both the United States and the UK. Well done "BRITAIN TRUMP"!' it reads.

Since President JD Vance's inauguration earlier in the year, rumours have swirled that Donald Trump's ill health has not lessened his influence over the White House nor his love of late-night social media binges. In Moscow, it is a more reasonable hour for diplomacy and Russia's Ministry of Foreign Affairs posts a rare message of congratulations to Britain on the election of a 'courageous' new leader.

6.15 a.m.

The humiliations for staff at Labour HQ are not over yet.

'Labour's Party Political Broadcast had been heavily criticised during the campaign and I think I can spot its star beside Nigel Farage in the audience there,' Chris Mason says. 'Yes, that's right, that's her.' He allows himself a brief chortle as he watches the live pictures from GB News.

'Sally's Birthday' told the story of a 10-year-old schoolgirl who had broken her wrist falling from a tree. In one storyline, she had an operation within days in a National

Health Service hospital where, as a doctor told viewers in a speech walking through the streets of east London, waiting lists were down and new drugs were available. In the other storyline, Sally was treated in a privatised NHS, meaning her parents had to choose between buying a birthday present for their daughter and paying for her healthcare without resorting to a buy-now-pay-later loan. But while waiting lists had come down, they were still far higher than under the previous Labour government. There was a backlash when the health secretary went on ITV's *Good Morning Britain* and declared hospitals were the 'best they'd ever been'. Nigel Farage had neutralised the attacks on his former remarks suggesting an insurance-based system for the NHS in an emotional interview with Piers Morgan about how the health service had saved his life when he had testicular cancer, backtracking on previous comments that he was almost killed by the 'incompetence and negligence' of the NHS. The Labour broadcast even drew criticism from JD Vance, who took it as an attack on America's own insurance-based system. The media circus which ensued dominated the conversation for at least three days in the crucial final week of the election and placed a question mark in the minds of many voters on Labour's trustworthiness when it came to the nation's health.

And now the star of the show, dressed in a Union Jack dress, was being held aloft by Farage and kissed on the cheek at the victory party while her beaming father and mother looked on.

6.20 a.m.

There was plenty of champagne ready for the champions at GB News to toast Farage's victory speech. Nick Candy, the Party's multi-millionaire property developer treasurer, had worked his magic on the dismal newsroom and had marshalled the Party's long list of donors, many of them his friends in the City, to cough up for 'Nige's coronation'. The days of the 'smoked salmon offensive' when Labour Chancellor of the Exchequer Rachel Reeves wooed big business before the 2024 election seemed very long ago. The City had welcomed Farage back in from the cold and his former trading partners joined him for dinners to reminisce about the old days and donate to Reform.

At Farage's speeches, the audience was increasingly filled with Tufton Street think-tank people and banking lobbyists. In 2025, Reform's deputy leader and then economic spokesperson Richard Tice gave a speech to Bloomberg that was regarded as a pitch to the City, arguing as it did for Thatcher-style deregulation to make London a leading centre for international capital again. This helped to gently reassure the titans of financial services that, come a Farage premiership, they would have nothing to worry about. The chancellor seized on Farage's cosying up to big business as sowing the seeds of the next financial crisis, arguing it amounted to 'reckless greed' that would only harm the British people. This delighted Labour's base, but sent another red alert to floating voters on Reform's list of target seats. The feeling was encouraged by a new wealth tax, which put an annual levy of 2 per cent on wealth in excess of £10 million: despite not being affected at all by the changes, this made voters in places like Cambridge, Twickenham and Tunbridge Wells flock back to the Liberal Democrats, fearing the tax would be extended to their own investments and pensions. Splitting the left voting bloc had proved another gift to Reform.

Also at GB News, but firmly off-camera, is the chair of the Confederation of British Industry. A staunch Europhile, he had clashed privately with Farage during the Brexit referendum and the CBI had been one of the most vocal business backers of the Remain campaign. But that was well over a decade ago now and his members had grown sick and tired of the broken promises for more growth under Labour. The chairman had had private dinners with CBI members, some of the country's biggest employers, who told him that Britain somehow managed to combine the worst of both worlds after the last decade, with more tariffs on British goods destined for the European Union and the United States, coupled with a European level of workers' protections that made hiring anyone more expensive and firing them much harder. Farage had made some eye-catching promises in the campaign: the Britannia Card, a £250,000 visa in exchange for favourable tax status to bring the wealthy international elite back to London and loosening restrictions on bosses' pay deals. Maybe Tice really could bring British businesses' mojo back, they wondered. It would have been impossible to come out forcefully for Reform during the election, but the CBI did not condemn Farage nor back the government and relations were getting warmer by the day. The chairman had even exchanged the odd friendly WhatsApp with the Reform leader. Relations were so good that when party donor Christopher Harborne invited him along to the victory party, he saw it as the perfect networking opportunity.

6.25 a.m.

A brown envelope is handed to Farage to read while he takes a break from interviews in the green room. Its contents are the work of a team of Reform Research Department staffers holed up in a Westminster hotel for the last two weeks. 'If we're going to do something big, we need to do it immediately,' Farage had told them at a dinner to mark the start of their work. In 1997, Labour Chancellor Gordon Brown had commanded his economic advisor Ed Balls to do the same before they made the Bank of England independent on their first day in office. Farage had requested to be alone as he studied the contents of the plan.

6.45 a.m.

Farage takes a call from PM Giorgia Meloni, who was re-elected in Italy two years earlier, to offer her congratulations. Few would have expected it, but Farage has changed and so has Reform. Only recently, the owner of Boisdale's moaned to a journalist that his favourite customer no longer spent his Thursday evenings enjoying single malts and haggis at his tables. The BBC ran the story, but it was helpful coverage as it spoke to Farage's general strategy: appear sober, sensible and ready for government. This meant fewer silly photographs for the press outside the Westminster Arms, grinning with a pint. He also ceased the Party's association with British cardiologist Aseem Malhotra, an anti-vaxxer who had claimed at the 2025 Reform Party conference that jabs had given the royal family cancer. A profile in the *New Yorker* noted: 'Farage has shown he can play Falstaff, Shakespeare's drunken reveller. But now he must play Feste – entertaining, always, but clever and ruthless too'.

The turn had been inspired by a trip to Rome to meet with Meloni and her advisors, where Farage had sipped spumante looking out over the Palatine and discussed how she had gone from dynamic right-wing outsider to kingmaker in Europe. As Meloni predicted, the more self-consciously serious style had meant Farage's message was more widely heard and respected: when a migrant was accidentally released from a detention camp and charged with burning down the St Anselm parish hall in Essex around Easter, Farage had conducted an emotional interview on GB News with the local women who relied on it. He was nominated for his third national TV award.

Rather than seem opportunistic, more and more people had seen him as a sensible politician who they believed could run the country and enjoy a pint. It was a far cry from five years earlier when Farage had criticised the Church for being too 'woke': his religious advisors, James Orr and Danny Kruger, had convinced him that being seen to attend services would soften his image. He stayed friendly with the Christians, following advice from the evangelical co-owner of GB News, Paul Marshall, and was filmed in Tunbridge Wells on a Sunday wearing tweed and serving bowls of soup to the homeless.

Marshall's advice was particularly appreciated since he had become a Reform donor in 2028. When Farage's former local, The Rifleman, was earmarked for conversion into luxury flats, he led a campaign to save it, using the community buy-out function. 'Che Farage Saves Local,' ran the headline in *Kent Online*. Farage's youngest daughter Isabelle, a 24-year-old former staffer at the US House of Representatives, joined his team and started appearing in his TikToks, taking part in trends and getting him to react to comments under his old European Parliament videos on YouTube. One of Farage's grandchildren said he was 'just a great grandpa' to an ITV reporter when the family were heading to the Christmas service at St Anselm's. The transformation was seemingly complete.

6.50 a.m.

Former Secretary of State for Energy Security and Net Zero Ed Miliband narrowly hangs on in Doncaster North, despite Reform throwing everything at the seat. When a shock power outage caused Addenbrooke's hospital in Cambridge to rely on emergency generators, Farage had rushed to stand beneath some local turbines, blaming Miliband's 'net zero agenda'. But instead of using the language of fanaticism and wokery, he blamed net zero for putting national security at risk and bills up.

During the blazing summer, with several days reaching 40°C or more, air conditioning and Britain's lack of it had become a major issue at the election. It had been driven to the top of the news agenda after the tragic death of a former Olympian due to overheating on the hottest day of the year. The Labour government led a campaign to promote 'alternative forms of cooling' such as new design rules on housebuilders and advice on drinking enough water. Farage had made hay with the announcements. 'We've just had a bit of really quite good weather for once,' Farage told press while licking an ice cream on Clacton pier. 'But we have to put up with this constant government scare-mongering. Put factor 75 all over your body. Wear a burqa. You'd have thought we'd never had a summer before!' He was wearing a baseball cap made by a fan saying 'Feel the Burn', with a picture of Andy Burnham, who had been vocal about the need for action on climate change, mocked up to look like the devil on fire. The hats became a hit on the left and were resold for hundreds of pounds on eBay.

6.51 a.m.

At the BBC studios in Elstree, the commentators on the panel had changed. Dan Sambrook[7], a freelance commentator and a contributor to the far-right *Pimlico Journal* Substack credited with giving intellectual heft to Reform, sits beside a columnist for the *Guardian*, the re-elected Reform MP for Romford Andrew Rosindell, a reporter for the *Daily Express,* and a newly elected Green MP for Stroud, the entrepreneur, philanthropist and climate campaigner Dale Vince.

---

[7]Dan Sambrook is one of a few fictional inventions designed for illustrative purposes.

'I think we can say that people are waking up this morning to a very different Britain,' says Sambrook. He had just filed his latest anonymous piece for the *Journal*, which now had 150,000 subscribers. Sambrook and his colleagues had gone from filming migrant boats landing in Kent at university to being invited to the *Spectator* summer garden party, all in a couple of short years. Now the *Pimlico Journal* is frequently quoted on strategist Dominic Cummings' own Substack and even bookers for BBC panels are starting to take notice.

'While the chattering classes have been focused on those ridiculous rallies, there has been a quiet, democratic coup against an establishment which has ruled this country for over 30 years. If I was the Cabinet Secretary right now, if I was a Supreme Court judge right now, if I was an illegal immigrant right now, if I was the Bank of England Governor right now, if I was a civil servant in a failing department right now, I wouldn't be sleeping. This country has seen the cancer you've allowed to spread and enacted a revolution via the ballot box.'

'If I was Nigel Farage and I'd just accidentally become Prime Minister, I'd be worried too,' the *Guardian* columnist jokes.

'The UK after Blair is like a horror show where a sadistic doctor prescribes the most self-rapacious, neoliberal medicine you can possibly design to a country already sick with the most hard left, cultural Marxist open-door migration system imaginable,' Sambrook says.[8] He speaks with a trained purpose at odds with the upbeat tone of the broadcast studio. His pale face and blue eyes, crowned with perfectly combed hair, betray no expression.

'It then starts battery farming terrorists and locking up anyone who wants to feel a sense of national pride outside of sport. Just look at Lucy Connolly, Stockport, the

---

[8]Cultural Marxism is a term used on the right to describe left-wing ideology which it is claimed is seeking to undermine Western values.

Manchester synagogue attack ... Reform is probably our last chance to avoid a civil war.'

The columnist snorts and tries to interrupt: 'That's a ridiculous racist conspiracy theory ...'

'Let him speak,' interjects a *Daily Express* reporter, who has recently been reprimanded by his newspaper for demanding proof of a Muslim MP's citizenship during a press conference. He is hopeful Sambrook can put in a word for him with Farage about a job in his No 10 media operation.

'To you liberals, everyone is racist, so it doesn't mean much, does it?' Sambrook scoffs, before ploughing on. 'I'd like to see Nigel demolish as much of the sclerotic liberal Blairite bureaucracy as possible, starting with the Supreme Court. Whatever it takes. Junk the ECHR [European Convention on Human Rights], disapply the Refugee Convention 1951 and repeal the Human Rights Act 2001.'

'Quite right,' says the Reform MP. 'This is what my constituents voted for tonight.'

'Cut disability benefits to incentivise work. Scrap Net Stupid Zero and shutter its building on Whitehall ...'

'You should be ashamed of yourself,' Vince says.

'Replace it with the Department of Government Efficiency,' Sambrook continues. 'Danny Kruger is right, we must drain the Whitehall swamp. We ran an empire with hundreds of millions of subjects out of an office containing like 26 people. Why can't we do it today? Probably there are too many low-IQ civil servants to manage it.'

All the guests speak at once and the presenter is caught in the crossfire but Sambrook isn't finished.

'Scrap the DEI [Division, Equity and Inclusion] agenda, hand out actual prison sentences for petty crime and stop taxing British families on low wages, for God's sake! But most important of all is Nigel's mission to de-Islamify Britain. We need to take the firmest possible measures to smash the ghettos that have sprung up countrywide,' he declares.

WHAT IF REFORM WINS

Andrew Rosindell lets out a thin, uncomfortable laugh beside him. The BBC interviewer prevaricates. The broadcaster had received the highest number of complaints in its history about its coverage of Reform during the general election, with those on the left furious at perceived bias towards Farage's party and what they considered to be its misleading and spurious claims. The interviewer asks the MP what he thinks the key moments in the election were.

'Sorry, but just before I answer that, I want to say that's certainly not Reform policy. We do not associate with Dan's remarks on that at all.' He looks to his side nervously, unsure whether he has been firm enough. 'In terms of what the key moments were, for us we saw a huge bump in support in Northern areas for our grooming gangs push. The optics of Nigel standing on a stage in Rotherham with 50 grooming gang victims, some of whom had never come forward before, was a sight to behold. I want to pay tribute to Ellie Reynolds, our incredible shadow social services minister, for organising that. Labour have overseen an epidemic of sexual violence on our streets at the hands of Pakistani gangs and fighting-age men coming here on boats. The media didn't cover it, so we put it on the agenda. It's a scandal and people responded to it – we saw our vote solidify in the so-called red wall considerably after that, which was very pleasing.'

6.55 a.m.

The newly elected MP for Aberdeen South, Stephen Flynn, has just won his seat with a 5 per cent swing to the SNP, but he doesn't look happy about it.

'Mr Flynn, I thought you would be delighted to have won so handsomely this morning. Your party have had an excellent night. What's your reaction?' asks the BBC's Nick

Robinson, who has taken over the morning's coverage from Clive Myrie and Laura Kuenssberg.

'What parties in Westminster, not just Reform, have to understand is that the mandate now for the SNP to hold a referendum on independence is irrefutable. Our leader John Swinney outlined at the start of our election campaign that in the event of a Reform majority in England and Wales, and a SNP majority in Scotland, we would be calling for an immediate referendum on independence. Scotland will be governed not for the first time in its history by a party that has no democratic mandate north of the border …'

'Hang on a second,' Robinson says, 'Reform have surged to second place in Scotland and have picked up MPs all over the country.'

'Nick, are you seriously telling me that Nigel Farage getting 11 MPs from Scotland in Parliament compared to the SNP getting 45 means anything? As I was saying, our voters went into the ballot box yesterday in the full understanding that a vote for the SNP was a vote for another vote on independence – we now have the strongest democratic mandate for a referendum since 2014. The Scottish people are speaking more forcefully now than ever – we do not want a racist, xenophobic government which is about to have another clash with the EU and repeal the Human Rights Act as our overlords.'

6.59 a.m.

Over on 12 Millbank, the headquarters of MI5, the Director General brings up the new prime minister's file on his desktop. It is one of the longest the service has on serving politicians: there are sections on everything from girlfriends from his teenage years, and where he gets his hair cut, to his various houses and businesses. There is one marked simply 'Foreign'. On his phone, the DG sees a push notification from the BBC: 'Watch live as Britain's next prime minister arrives at Downing Street'. He scrolls to a part of the document only he has access to and confirms the document's permanent deletion. Now that Nigel Farage is Prime Minister and has oversight of the secret state, the DG has no desire to make new enemies in high places.

In this scenario, Nigel Farage is now hours away from occupying No 10 Downing Street. Everything that could have gone right for Reform has, as a broad coalition of the centre and left either came too late or failed to emerge. The UK has been dominated by Labour and Tories for so long that in some ways alliances between parties are anathema to the nation's political DNA. It doesn't help that on the few occasions in history where parties have joined forces to form a government outside of wartime, it has decimated one of them – when the Liberals supported Labour's first minority government in 1924, it destroyed them, and when the Lib Dems formed a coalition with the Tories in 2010, it sent them out into political obscurity. The Brexit Party won no seats in 2019 when Farage himself made a deal with the Conservatives. The failure even led him to briefly 'retire' from frontline politics. But in a startling twist of fate ten years later, with the two-party system in ruins, Farage has emerged out of the wilderness and into the halls of power.

2

Victory

Friday, 29 June 2029

7 a.m.

From the moment they achieve a majority in the Commons, the arms of the British secret state close around a prime minister. A heavily bomb-proofed Audi A8 L and trained drivers from the Royalty and Specialist Protection branch will replace Farage's car and will not leave his side until he steps down from office. The officers will be specialists in anti-hijacking manoeuvres and evasive driving at speed. He will be surrounded by a police motorcade wherever he goes. This is the car that Nigel Farage will now take from GB News to Westminster.

Before he is allowed to enter, a party photographer sets up a photo for Farage and his wife Laure kissing in a 'private' moment. 'The next First Couple of Britain,' reads the Fox News banner as Farage gets into his new ride. A screenshot of the image goes viral on X.

There is time for a quick TikTok video for his fans. 'Well, folks! Isn't this crackers? Looks like we're on to blow the bloody doors off! Alarm clock Britain has finally woken up,' he tells his followers with a deep chuckle, the happy result of countless cigarettes.

'Britain has said bye-bye to Labour. It's said enough of importing illegal immigrants. It's said enough of their

WHAT IF REFORM WINS

taxes paying for 4-star hotels for God knows who. It's said enough of giving fighting-age males pocket money. Cheers!' he beams into the bright lights, taking a sip of his pint.

'Yep, that's good,' says the 20-year-old Reform cameraman. He clicks off the ringlight and Farage hands back the pint to his aide, who drinks it himself by the side of the road as the Audi speeds off into the dawn.[9]

9 a.m.

The largest police presence in history for the arrival of a new prime minister is out on show along Whitehall but that hasn't stopped signs of dissent. Protestors overnight have rushed to scrawl 'FASCISTS' in turquoise paint across the walls of Horse Guards, the Ministry of Defence and the Cabinet Office. Reform's HQ at Millbank Tower has had the same treatment and its ground-floor windows are kicked in. If you were to stand where Trafalgar Square meets Whitehall, the road gently sloping down towards Westminster, you would see a thin fluorescent line of officers separating Pride and orange and black Refugee flags on one side, and a sea of St George crosses on the other.

A carnival of Britain's far-right have turned up: activist Tommy Robinson on a stage near the Women of the Second World War Memorial, calling Farage a 'cultural Marxist'; the equestrian statue of Earl Haig has been festooned with a turquoise Hawaiian garland by the Reform-supporting porn star Bonnie Blue, while Liz Truss, having been rejected

---

[9] The importance to Farage of feeding the social media beast cannot be overstated. In an interview after stepping back from politics, before he came back to lead Reform, he said that he had more influence on GB News and TikTok than he would have as MP for Clacton.

VICTORY

by Farage for a shadow cabinet role, is looking into the crowd outside the Ministry of Defence for the GB News producer who promised to interview her.

10.20 a.m.

The door of No 10 Downing Street opens and the outgoing prime minister approaches the podium placed opposite the media.

'Good morning. I will shortly be seeing His Majesty The King to offer my resignation as Prime Minister. To all the Labour colleagues and campaigners who are disappointed today, I'm sorry we couldn't have done more. I know you will be feeling shocked and worried this morning – the world feels like a darker place. You ran a wonderful campaign and we must rebuild.'

The prime minister goes on to list the party's achievements before warning that 'everything has been put at risk by a man who I believe has tricked Britain into taking a dark and uncertain path at a time when the world is more uncertain than ever.' Loud boos and the sound of drums cause them to lose momentum. They thank the appropriate people and supporters before their car door opens, the motorcade is prepared and they are sped away to Buckingham Palace.

11.40 a.m.

When it looks as if the battle for Downing Street has been won, the King's private secretary will call the 'prime minister-designate', informing them to stand by for a request to come to the Palace for the 'kissing of hands' ceremony. Courtiers block off 11 a.m. and midday in His Majesty's diary on the Friday after the vote to perform his constitutional function as head of state. His hands aren't actually kissed, with a brief bow and handshake in front of the cameras sufficient to acknowledge the monarch's invitation to the prime minister to form a government. Gone are the days when H.H. Asquith in 1908 took a ship and train from London to the French resort of Biarritz to brush the hands of Edward VII with his lips and accept his invitation to form a Liberal administration.

The kissing of the hands is an ancient symbol of sovereign authority, and speculation is rife that Charles could bring his constitutional powers back to life and block a Farage premiership. Experts are hounded by journalists trying to understand the ramifications of such a scenario: Andrew Blick, Professor of Politics and Contemporary History at King's College London, is on the BBC, outlining how the usual position is that the monarch asks 'the person who appears most likely to be able to command the confidence of the house of Commons'. In theory, this gives the King an option on who to call. However, Blick warns the last time the monarch selected a British prime minister of his own choosing was in 1834, when William IV dismissed Lord Melbourne from his post, and even then it was widely regarded as having caused him embarrassment. This does not stop armchair experts online from saying that while Farage has achieved a majority, if the King refused to ask Farage to the Palace, maybe he could be stopped. Many in the country are still in denial that a man like Farage could be PM. Charles has so far stayed out of politics during his reign, they concede, but at a moment when the environmental cause is at risk from a party intent on ripping up net zero legislation, surely this is one time he could be persuaded to act.

The sight of Farage's car hastening down the Mall puts paid to any hopes that the King might break with centuries of convention. It is less clear, Blick warns, if Farage feels the same sense of duty.

The outgoing minister is stripped of the trappings of office immediately: they are not filmed as they make a private exit at the back of the Palace in their own car after their audience. Whereas in America a change of government takes 11 weeks, in Britain it is almost immediate. In 2016, just 32 seconds separated David Cameron's car leaving the Palace and Theresa May's entering. For the prime minister-designate, it was once normal to arrive in their private vehicle, but recently leaders have been placed immediately under security protection and use the government Audi.

Farage is greeted by Sir Clive Alderton, the King's private secretary, and Lieutenant Commander Will Thornton of the Fleet Air Arm, the King's equerry, and ushered through the Palace's gilded halls to a chair in an antechamber near the King's private apartments. This is where the Lord Chamberlain, Lord Richard Benyon, arrives to meet Farage before the audience. Benyon has strong views on Europe – when he was an MP, he was expelled by the Conservative Party for voting to try to stop a no-deal Brexit – but these will be put aside as he briefs Farage on the audience. 'You may be surprised at the King's condition. He has slowed down rather a lot in recent months, so go gently and speak up,' he warns.

The Audience Room is decorated with a large painting of the City from Somerset House by Canaletto, a pair of porcelain pheasants on the mantelpiece and a photograph of William and Kate's engagement. What happens inside is guarded with secrecy. For the photo to mark the occasion, Charles struggles up from the settee and stands upright, his eyes sunken and red as he asks Farage to form an administration. 'Yes, sir,' comes the reply. At that moment, as Harold Wilson said in 1964, Farage becomes Prime Minister of Great Britain and Northern Ireland and First Lord of the Treasury 'on the spot'.

'When he led the charge to take Britain out of Europe in 2016, some said Farage was the most consequential political figure of our times to never hold office,' Nick Robinson is telling viewers on the BBC. 'On his election to Downing Street, he is the most consequential of the last three decades, full stop and no questions asked. Farage, a man who failed to become an MP seven times, who was dismissed as leading a party of "fruit-cakes and loonies" by Cameron, who has survived scandal after scandal and accusations of racism, is being asked right now by the monarch to form a government in his name. He will lead the world's sixth biggest economy, a country with significant international military and security operations. He and his party have eliminated the one-hundred-year-old political consensus that, no matter what, either the reds or the blues will rule. In 2029, Britain has turned turquoise.'

In the Audience Room, Charles, in a hoarse voice, asks Farage what his plans for government are. Gordon Brown described a similar chat with the Queen as 'a congenial business-like conversation about the work that lay ahead'. But behind the closed doors of the audience room, there is plenty of room for royal interference. Contrary to popular belief, the monarch is allowed to express opinions to the prime minister and influence them. As the journalist and essayist Walter Bagehot wrote in 1867, the monarch has 'the right to be consulted, the right to encourage, the right to warn'.[10] Afterwards, Farage's team give a readout to the lobby that the prime minister 'had a laugh' with the King over their shared love of fly fishing and memories of a visit Charles made to the European Commission. But Charles characterises the conversations very differently to Richard Benyon afterwards: after discussing the natural beauty of Kent's

---

[10] The journalist and essayist is credited with defining the constitutional role of the modern monarchy in his work *The English Constitution*.

chalk stream rivers, royal eyebrows were raised when Farage mentioned the billions to be made from nearby shale gas fracking projects, which his party are keen to green-light.

After the audience, courtiers provide a room for the new prime minister to reflect on their new position and to polish a draft of a speech to be given in front of Downing Street. Farage moves his chair closer to the heater in the corner as he writes – even though it's a sunny morning in July, Buckingham Palace is notoriously draughty. He is then escorted down the Palace's 'Minister's Staircase' by Benyon and Alderton and heads to the prime ministerial car. The first sign of Farage's new status is that the two men address him as 'Prime Minister'. The second will be the salute given by the guards as he makes his way to the waiting car. He begins the journey east.

11.50 a.m.

The BBC cameraman on Downing Street pans left and the country glimpses the tribe set to govern them, arranged along the pavement. They take selfies in front of the famous door. A couple who work together as advisors even share a snog beside the railings for their Instagram. Someone is holding a GoPro camera on a stick, broadcasting everything on the live streaming site Twitch. Gone are the Charles Tyrwhitt suits of the Starmer days. For the older members of Farage's entourage, large white cuffs, bulky watches, whitened teeth and baggy suit trousers draped over black Oxfords are in order. Turquoise ties abound, of course. The odd-and-sods collection of younger members is comprised of a junior advisor taken from the Party's youth wing with a six-inch wide handlebar moustache, a nephew of Tucker Carlson with a deep Florida tan, and a couple of young women wearing Burberry trench coats tied neatly around their waists. There's a smattering of Barbours.

After the 2024 election, a significant minority of Labour No 10 SpAds (special advisors) didn't even know if they were definitely going to have jobs in the new government and the same is true for those gathered on Downing Street now. But that doesn't mean the civil servants, also known as officials, inside haven't done their homework on who's who: when staffers arrive at their desks on the first day, the civil servants may have already researched which universities they went to and where they are from.

The Downing Street protection team will also be prepared: the head of security puts a meeting in all of their calendars to quiz them about which countries they've visited, especially China or Russia. They will also be given a presentation on all the ways foreign spy agencies could try and infiltrate sensitive conversations and documents: during a first-week briefing for Labour aides in 2024, one department's head of security demonstrated the ease with which they could be surveilled by hiding a camera in a bottle and a bug in a USB drive.

But that was all for them to worry about next week: for tonight, there is a plan afoot to hit another Reform party at the National Liberal Club for the free drinks, then on to the Marquis of Granby in Pimlico for old times' sake before heading to Scott's in Mayfair for a late private dinner. They will spend Saturday hungover and wait nervously by their phones for a call.

12.10 p.m.

The noise of the broadcast helicopter thunders overhead as Farage's car passes the Wales Office on the west side of Whitehall. A new lectern is placed outside No 10.

'A Reform scriptwriter could barely have dreamt of this,' Myrie says. 'Farage is prime minister and the sun has come out.' Pointing to the flags of Wales, Scotland and England held by Farage's political allies, Myrie informs his viewers, Reform 'are the largest party in Wales and have picked up seats in Scotland. It gives Farage enormous political power if he can hold his untested party together.' The BBC editor in charge briefly cuts to Clacton pier, where hundreds of supporters are holding a party in the sunshine. The camera tracks Farage's car as he heads past Horse Guards. 'This journey, which has felt so hard, so impossible for Farage, is finally at an end,' Myrie says.

From nowhere an indistinguishable round projectile flies overhead. Shards of shell and orange yolk slide down the passenger window. A second later, out of the blue a strawberry milkshake arrives and explodes across the windscreen. Through blackout windows, paparazzi manage to catch a glimpse of Farage's disgusted reaction as he pulls into his new address.

12.15 p.m.

The gates of Downing Street swing open for the 60th prime minister of Great Britain and Northern Ireland. His car swoops in from Whitehall: as a member of security opens the door to Farage and his wife Laure, an almighty gust of booing and whooping thunders through the narrow Georgian street. A bank of photographers compete for a shot of the new leader beside the milkshake covering the tinted windows of the government car. As he makes his way towards the famous black door, this is the new PM's opportunity to thank in person the many people who have been working hard on their behalf. Wearing a froglike grin, Farage approaches the ecstatic tribe of shadow ministers, family, advisors and bag carriers, who chant, 'Nigel! Nigel! Nigel!'

as he shakes the hands of Richard Tice, soon to be officially appointed Chancellor of the Exchequer, and Zia Yusuf, who despite losing his seat has been drafted in as head of the Policy Unit in No 10. Arron Banks, who has supported him as far back as his UKIP days, is singled out for a manly slap on the back. Suella Braverman, Lee Anderson, Andrea Jenkyns and Danny Kruger are beaming; all are confident that they will be joining Farage around the Cabinet table. Robert Jenrick stands at the side, applauding dutifully.

12.18 p.m.

Farage walks hand in hand with Laure up the street, surrounded on all sides by supporters, before approaching the lectern. Elections are bruising and divisive for any country, and prime ministers often use the moment to bring people together during their first address to the nation. He says he had been asked by the King to form a government, pays tribute to the British public for putting their trust in Reform and to the former prime minister for conceding. So far, so statesman-like. But then Farage's tone shifts: 'For too long, the people of this country have been abused by the men and women who have occupied the residence behind me. They've lied to you, served their own interests. They made a choice: to prioritise importing illegals instead of the security of Britain. That ends today.'

In this scenario, Farage seizes the opportunity – with the world watching – to reveal what will be his signature policy and vision for the country.

'My government will today undertake a series of measures to free us from the overreach of a foreign power. We will submit a letter to the Council of Europe immediately requesting withdrawal from the European Court of Human Rights. We will also disapply the Refugee Convention.'

The aides outside No 10 know that this will trigger a year-long process, during which time the Reform government plans to introduce legislation into Parliament for a Great Repeal Bill to remove the Human Rights Act from the statute books. This will be replaced with a British Bill of Rights based on English common law, with specific measures to ensure it is not, in the parlance of the party, 'abused by judges and migrants attempting to stay in this country'.

Farage is still speaking: 'We will abolish indefinite leave to remain and begin issuing five-year visas to those who wish to come here legally. We will ramp up detention capacity to 24,000 spaces.[11] Politicians in Westminster have profited, while the people suffered the consequences of uncontrolled migration: migrant hotels, rampant crime and rotting public services. Enough is enough! Reform will finally get a grip on the population crisis and enact the will of the people, who have shown there is a majority for common sense in the country.'

'My home secretary will have a legal obligation to deport illegal migrants and will have the means, through new deportation units, to fulfil that duty. Once we have exited the Human Rights Act and the ECHR, we will be able to send in the Navy to repel and remove illegal migrants coming via the Channel at will. My government will work on behalf of you, not the bloated Civil Service, left-wing lawyers or Channel migrants. We expect these measures to bring immigration down to thousands. There will be a backlash from the establishment as we deliver our manifesto: the eco-lobby, the BBC, the House of Lords, the judges. They will throw everything at us to prevent this elected government from carrying out a Reform manifesto, but we will never surrender.'

All the Reform aides have stopped waving their flags and are listening intently.

---

[11] From a base of 2,200 in 2024.

'I promise to restore pride back to this great country, which once led the world but has fallen so far from its glorious history. We will defund the BBC and hold it to account, we will scrap net zero, bring down bills and safeguard our energy security. There is a mountain to climb. It will not always be easy and it's going to be a devil of a job – there will be painful decisions before we can get on the right footing to make work pay and our country prosperous once more. We are a new government, there will be some hiccups, but I want you to remember that as we make our first steps in Downing Street, we are one nation, one family, one community. I will never forget that when I walk through that door. Thank you.'

12.20 p.m.

The figure who had helped write the speech looks on from a window high in Downing Street. As in 2019 when he served Boris Johnson, he'd already let himself in through a back entrance to be there for his boss's entrance. Despite the many late-night WhatsApps exchanged with Farage over the past three years, the relationship until now was not official: Dominic Cummings was even a little surprised when he got the call last month. It had started when he went for a secret dinner with Farage in December 2024, where in his words they discussed 'the core problems are that we have a broken Whitehall, a disgraceful and shattered Tory Party clogging up the party system'.

The pair had had their differences. Farage even once called him a 'horrible little man'. Cummings' Vote Leave campaign beat Farage's Grassroots Out to be the official Eurosceptic campaign during the Brexit referendum, but they are both driven by a conviction that the freedoms they fought for in 2016 have been squandered.[12] Farage needs Cummings' insights into what Reform is up against, while Cummings has unfinished business in SW1. From a little cottage on Holy Island in Lindisfarne, Northumberland, Cummings had perfected a plan for what a Reform government could do to transform Britain. Now he was back in Downing Street, he had the opportunity to make the political weather once more.

12.23 p.m.

If they can command a majority in the House of Commons, a British prime minister has almost no hard constraints on their power. Farage, acting on behalf of the Crown via the royal prerogative, can, for example, take Britain to war without the consent of Parliament, which has no constitutional role in the process. Although since the vote on intervention in Iraq in 2003 a convention has arisen that a PM will seek the consent of the Commons before taking such action, it is still just a convention. There is, however, a fine matrix of informal checks and balances around the prime minister. One of these is the role of cabinet ministers who, in practice, Farage needs to run the government. A renowned control freak, the new PM has plans to compile a cabinet of MPs, donors, supporters in the press, and business executives designed to be subservient. His quickest way to bring in outside appointments is via the Lords: just as Rishi Sunak did with Lord Cameron when he made the former prime minister Foreign Secretary, Farage elevates Andrea Jenkyns, who has just stepped down as Lincolnshire's mayor, to serve as Secretary of State for Energy. Reform had originally planned to combine the Business, Trade and

---

[12]Despite spending over a year as the chief advisor to Boris Johnson, the PM who saw through the Brexit deal.

Energy departments, but turned against the idea when they realised the scale of the task it would be to dismantle net zero. Farage also ennobled Kevin Byrne, the founder of Checkatrade.com, to a ministerial position at Business and Trade. But even if he chooses carefully, loyalty is never certain and a prime minister cannot order a minister to do anything.[13] Prime ministers also need to keep their ministers, who have actual legal power and control over budgets in a way the PM doesn't, on side to achieve their policy objectives. The importance of their role was clear in September 2022 when a mass resignation of ministers brought about the end of the Boris Johnson government.

The second line of constitutional defence is the cabinet secretary, the prime minister's most senior policy advisor and head of the Civil Service. The chief guard of Britain's unwritten constitution, they form one corner of the 'Golden Triangle' of key officials to the prime minister, along with the principal private secretary and private secretary to the monarch. Given that the cabinet secretary has usually served the previous administration for years before the arrival of a new party, they are often seen with immediate suspicion by the incoming team. In 2025, this is how senior figures in No 10 viewed Sir Chris Wormald before he stood down in February the following year.

'You don't really need [a cabinet secretary],' one government source said, describing Wormald in the months before his departure as 'ineffective'. In this scenario, the incumbent cabinet secretary is about to greet Farage when he walks through the portal and into the black-and-white tiled hall of Downing Street.

In the two minutes before Farage enters, the cabinet secretary bounds down Downing Street's yellow Grand Staircase two steps at a time, past photos of Sunak, Starmer

---

[13] Though of course they can overrule them and ask for their resignation.

and Truss. They take a shortcut through the warren of small rooms and corridors connecting the seventeenth-century townhouse, commanding officials to come to the entrance hall to clap the new arrival.

Downing Street is a thoroughly impractical and 'surprisingly unglamorous' place from which to run a modern nation, its labyrinthine design preventing easy communication and encouraging mystery and intrigue. Away from the Georgian state rooms downstairs, teams are siloed into tiny offices. To aide collaboration, doors are usually left open, but this makes it paradoxically easier to covertly stand behind a door and eavesdrop. In the attic meeting rooms, who is going into which room with whom is closely surveilled. Nearly three years into the job, the cabinet secretary still notices the frayed curtains, the plastic Pret wrapper dropped in the Cabinet Room, the dust on the gold frames of the oil paintings: it's a shabbier place than when they first visited under Tony Blair. Successive prime ministers have delayed renovations – if they ask, they're told it would take four years and they might not be in office long enough to see the results.

Liz Truss found the place a 'soulless cage – with fleas' during her short stay, but even at the zenith of British imperial power, Benjamin Disraeli thought it 'dingy and decaying'. Those familiar with the flat above No 10 describe it as 'awful', with the one above No 11 only marginally better. Starmer 'hates the building and takes no joy in [thinking] "oh, I'm in Downing Street,"' according to those close to the PM. Like Slough House in the TV spy thriller *Slow Horses*, advisors tell of coffee stains on the carpet, dozens of people working in the dingy basement and a 'notoriously shit' café. Little wonder that during Tony Blair's early days as PM, moving out of No 10 completely, decamping the whole operation to the Queen Elizabeth Conference Centre opposite Westminster Abbey and creating an 'Office of the Prime Minister' was seriously considered as a remedy to the building's issues. His team eventually decided it wasn't worth the fuss the move would create.

Although at least one person familiar with the building sees more than a bit of snobbery in the complaints: 'It is a working office. Being a bit grubby isn't necessarily something to be ashamed of.' However, even they admitted that the café was to be avoided and that the offerings at the Cabinet Office or Foreign Office were better.

A few officials, former Fast Streamers in their mid-thirties, are crying at their desks, having just clapped out the former prime minister. The cabinet secretary gathers who they can. A few people line up on each side of the chequerboard foyer as the door opens, their trickle of lacklustre applause mingling with distant chants from the protest still raging on Whitehall.

12.23 p.m.

Meanwhile, Sir Tony Blair, the leader who led Labour to three general election victories, is being interviewed in the BBC studio opposite Buckingham Palace: 'I think a very important message has been sent to leaders of all the parties with this result. It's clear that there's a new reality that we must all come to terms with.'

Behind the scenes, the Tony Blair Institute for Global Change is already working on a consultancy strategy it hopes to sell to the new government which promises to turn Britain into an AI superpower. A briefing from the Reform camp will later say there are 'no plans' to work with the former prime minister.

12.26 p.m.

Despite all the efforts directed at winning a Reform majority before the election, preparation for government meetings, also known as 'access talks', were prioritised by Farage to show they were ready for power. Access talks are traditionally supposed to offer a chance for parties to discuss confidentially their plans for government with senior civil servants. In 2025, those who remembered Labour's lack of preparation for government said that if Reform wanted to hit the ground running on entering office they would have to engage at least partly with the Civil Service before the election. Usually only the official Opposition are offered them, but this time the Tories were so far back in the polls that Reform had been invited in. They had come in handy: James Orr, the senior Farage advisor who had been chosen to lead them, had tipped off the media every time he had gone in and out of those nondescript south London buildings. Whitehall likes to keep access talks far away from the centre of power. But Farage is not interested in polite cups of tea: he wants shock and awe, for officials to be scared of their new ministers. He hadn't turned up to the talks, and Orr had broken them off after a perceived slight. He has spent the campaign promising to scrap departments and fire staff who insist on working from home, in order to save the taxpayer millions in efficiencies. These tactics will be his chief weapons for making the Civil Service bend to his will. When the cabinet secretary opens the door on the morning of Farage's victory, this is the first time they have met.

The Mandarin invites the new prime minister to see his new office, known by some administrations as 'the den'. On his left as he walks through the entrance hall is a corridor leading to Nos 11 and 12, and on the right is the communications department, the new stomping ground of Farage's director of communications, Dan Jukes, and his pirates, Ed Sumner and John Gill. In front of Farage there is a smaller, second hall, which leads via a corridor towards the Cabinet anteroom. This is where ministers and officials wait for opportunistic 'brush-bys' with the prime minister to solicit his approval for their plans and schemes. Beyond is the famous cabinet room and to the left at the end lies the prime minister's tiny study. It used to be bigger, but then Pitt the Younger decided he wished to enlarge the Cabinet room to accommodate more ministers around the table so the den had to shrink. In an adjoining room, there is space for the PM's inner circle and Farage has given some thought to this: he knows he needs Dan Jukes, 'Posh George' Cotterel and Arron Banks. Dominic Cummings will also have a chair, he decides, as well as the property developer Nick Candy. Farage's Downing Street is one of unabashed machismo.

As news of key appointments in No 10 filters out, classicist Mary Beard tweets that 'the gender imbalance of Farage's Downing Street is one to make even the most chauvinist Caesar proud'.

12.32 p.m.

Farage's men enter and fan around the prime minister. The cabinet secretary takes a seat in the middle of the horseshoe and begins to brief him on his initial responsibilities. Their voice is generous, simple and firm – a tone shaped over years of service. They decide to start with the basics. 'I'm the cabinet secretary. I am the head of the Civil Service. This is your principal private secretary. She's responsible for running your private office in Downing Street. We are here to give you advice and carry out your policy objectives. You will receive submissions in a red box. Submissions are things we need political sign-off from you on. Only the very most important decisions will end up in your box, we will sift the rest.' (The private office secretly called them the prime minister's 'homework'.) 'You can also direct us what to do, while we can give advice and tell you if we think something is a bad idea.'

This wasn't quite the full story. They were fluent in all the tactics officials used to forestall the misguided ideas of new ministers. Never refuse a request outright. Say we haven't run the numbers, there's no data, that it's not possible, it's too complicated, you'd get JRed [judicial reviewed] and it'll take six months or more'.

The threat of judicial reviews, where the government is taken to court and a judge rules on the lawfulness of a policy, is a particularly effective weapon officials can use to kill off an idea. This is achieved via a legal risk assessment: if civil servants have graded a policy as 'medium-high' that it will be deemed illegal in the courts, it takes a very brave advisor or minister to push ahead with it. If a bullish minister continues anyway and loses, it can have wide-ranging impacts across many other areas of policies. An example from December 2025 is illustrative: the Reform-led Kent County Council attempted to save millions of pounds by changing their practice on charging disabled individuals for their care, which led to thousands of people paying more. A judicial review was launched, but before a judgment was made, KCC backed down and was forced to make alterations to its proposals. In a legal context where departments feel assaulted by the threat of embarrassing defeats in the courts, the minister usually gives up through death by a thousand cuts. 'Good officials say, "We can make things work" rather than present endless problems,' one government source complained in 2025. The problem, in their view, was that 'Labour people don't say, "Shut the fuck up" when an official refuses to comply.' In 2029, however, Labour was quickly becoming a distant memory in Whitehall.

Farage remains silent, fumbles in his suit, takes out a Silk Cut cigarette and begins to puff. The crackle of the tobacco is the only noise. He smokes around 20 cigarettes a day. The last prime minister who smoked with the same enthusiasm was Harold Wilson over 60 years ago, although like Farage preferring G&Ts to beer, Wilson privately opted for Romeo y Julieta cigars rather than his ubiquitous pipe.

'Looking at my notes I made during your predecessor's induction...' the cabinet secretary continues, waving away the smell. Smoking in Downing Street was banned by Tony Blair in 2007, like everywhere else, but he is aware that Farage might welcome the fight and so decides in the moment to say nothing and plough on with more important matters. 'He asked for a briefing on key areas of concern before we discussed his political priorities. These were the state of the economy; public order, so prisons, police, riots; the state of our intelligence objectives; the status of vital public services; and our relationships with key foreign allies and enemies. There will also be a security briefing from our team here and your advisors should be careful of photographers trying to snap their documents when leaving the building. We should also run through your ministerial selections and I must give you briefings on living arrangements for you and Laure ...'

But Farage refuses to be briefed on anything requested by his predecessor and asks for all the living arrangements information to be sent to Laure's assistant. He does allow the cabinet secretary to present him with the decision on the nuclear deterrent. Every Trident nuclear submarine has a handwritten letter from the PM containing their orders in the event Britain is hit by a surprise strike. The commander goes to the safe, removes the letter and reads whether they should retaliate or not. Farage is not allowed to take into consideration the words of his predecessors. In administrations past, PMs may have been able to ask former holders of the office what they decided, but Farage entertains no such relationships. He writes the note and hands it back. No one will ever know what he has decided.

'There is a saying of Mrs. Thatcher's that you'd do well to remember,' Farage says. 'Advisors advise, ministers decide. I give the orders, you follow them, not the other way around.'

'Yes, it is my job to advise. But it is your job, in the first instance, to listen.'

They lock eyes across the room. Farage's pirates shift in their seats.

The cabinet secretary returns to his room in the Cabinet Office, leaving the prime minister to discuss ministerial appointments with his advisors. On his way, he gives a wide-eyed stare at the principal private secretary, the universal language in the Civil Service for 'what the fuck are these morons doing?'

The next morning, a story will run in *The Times* about 'strife' in No 10 over the cabinet secretary's 'working relationship' with Farage and how senior No 10 sources think him 'ineffectual' and 'addicted to Cabinet Office orthodoxy'. When the previous cabinet secretary, Simon Case, stepped down in 2024, for the first time the job description for a future candidate required the cabinet secretary to 'secure the confidence of the prime minister', giving any occupant of No 10 a convenient tool to use to rid them of a difficult individual. On BBC Radio 4's *World at One*, Tim Montgomerie, a Reform outrider, says there is 'ample precedent' for the briefing and Farage had a right to act after winning the election on a promise to the electorate to 'clear out Whitehall'.

'Ian Bancroft went to the stake in the 1980s for clashing with Thatcher, Bob Kerslake under David Cameron quit after a series of negative stories, and in the noughties, Tony Blair was more than happy to see the back of Richard Wilson. The apolitical Civil Service is a fiction. The officials know it, and so does Farage. This briefing follows in a fine tradition of cabinet secretaries clashing with ministers. We need officials who can get a grip of the new government and how the country is changing, not metropolitan elites still hankering for a return to the days of Tony and Gordon.'

The day after the negative briefing, with the press camped outside their house, the cabinet secretary will not be able to make it into work. They will receive an email that afternoon thanking them for their longstanding service which states that as part of the prime Minister's plans to 'streamline' the Cabinet Office, the role is no longer required. Attached are the documents outlining a severance payout of £500,000. There will be some fuss and upset from certain newspapers and political podcasts in the days following, but it will be soon forgotten in the flurry of other announcements.

1 p.m.

An unlikely assemblage of men in suits shuffles from the back of the British Museum's Enlightenment Gallery, past the reporters and behind three lecterns. Gordon Brown looks around him, seemingly surprised himself at how he's ended up here beside the other two. He spots the institution's chairman George Osborne, who has arranged the last-minute press conference, in the front row.

It is David Cameron who speaks first: 'Many thought this would never happen. And no, I'm not talking about Gordon Brown, John Major and me sharing a stage together. We never thought a populist right-wing force would seize control of the country we love. As former leaders of this great nation, we are unified in one clear message: this is not us, this is not the Britain we know, this is not the Britain we led. The language and proposed policies used by Nigel Farage in the campaign about migrants, about those on benefits and about his opponents has shocked us. We are announcing today that we are founding a non-profit organisation to act as a watchdog on our democratic rights and to guard against what is to come.'

It is the first time the 86-year-old John Major had has been seen in public for two years and he is using a walking stick. Gordon Brown looks pale, his head of white hair perched upon a baggy suit. Even David Cameron seems tired and is filmed shaking his head as he greets George Osborne after the speech.

Meanwhile, at Derry Street in South Kensington, the offices of the *Daily Mail*, editors had just received the judgement of another former prime minister. Boris Johnson could not fully support the new government, but in the face of Farage's victory it was now impossible to lambast the new prime minister like he'd done in other columns.

'Farage, if he can hold his party together, has pulled off a ballot box blinder. It's unclear what his rag-tag party of misfits will make of government, but I know one thing for sure – nothing can be worse than the socialist lunatics who have been running Downing Street in the last few years. He's scored early by putting Nadine Dorries back into the Cabinet. Britain has been ruled by po-faced HR managers for too long. In Farage, we have a Cavalier for a leader, not another irksome Roundhead. Maybe we'll see a repeal of the smoking ban. Having a flutter guilt-free. Pubs open till 1 a.m. I'll say cheers to that!'

1.03 p.m.

There is room in the Downing Street attic, which has been through so many uses officials have stopped bothering to name it. It once housed David Cameron's nanny, then was a Brexit crisis meeting room under May, before becoming the unlikely bedroom of Boris Johnson's mother-in-law. Someone said it had once been a mini-gym. It has one tiny sash window operated by a broken winch. Under Nigel Farage, it now houses four plastic chairs. On these sit the prime minister, his chancellor, his head of policy and Dominic Cummings, wearing a grey T-shirt, yellow

Converse and a beanie found on the floor of his son's bedroom. They had been summoned to the eyrie away from the private office downstairs to discuss their plan for what to do next, unsupervised. Cummings arrived first, the rest had been late: there is no map provided to newcomers in Downing Street for security reasons, so people are always getting lost. Farage is delighted with the splash his first speech is already making and giddy at the new reality of life at the top of the political ladder. They hear the sounds of the press still hoping for more drifting up from the street below.

Finally, alone without the cabinet secretary, they should have felt more relaxed, but old resentments still linger. Richard Tice and Zia Yusuf can't stand each other and are sitting in silence. Yusuf once insulted Tice's wife, the journalist Isabel Oakeshott, and he's never forgiven him.

Outside, the politicians' advisors are bickering. 'Where did you get that lanyard from?', one Yusuf advisor asks Tice's man. When a new administration enters Downing Street, they are informed by Security that what colour lanyard you possess denotes your clearance level and consequently whether you qualify for entry into the Downing Street bunker in the event of a nuclear attack. The only colour which gets you in is green, and Yusuf's man has orange.

'I work for the chancellor, of course I've got a green pass,' Tice's advisor says.

The SpAd makes a mental note to demand one from Security. Inside, Yusuf begins his presentation on the Policy Unit's agenda but is constantly interrupted by aggressive questions from Tice. He ceases his presentation, protesting that he cannot continue when he knows whatever he says will end up on the front page of the *Telegraph* the next day.

Tice storms out. Yusuf follows him out into the corridor, demanding to know whether Tice blocked him from getting a stand-up desk in his new office.

Dominic Cummings is the only person in the room with any experience of how government works and in this scenario, in the coming days and weeks, Farage is forced to turn to him. Later that day, Farage informs his private office in an email that anything coming from Cummings is coming directly from him. In his name, Cummings will set about rewiring first Downing Street, then the Civil Service, then the country itself.

Previous prime ministers have recognised the immediate importance of sweeping changes to their Downing Street operation: in 2022, within half an hour of Liz Truss becoming Prime Minister, she had cleared out Policy Unit civil servants from the second floor and had replaced them all with just four special advisors. They were banished to the Cabinet Office, many corridors away from the centre of power. One of the changes brought in under Cummings when he worked for Boris Johnson has had a surprisingly long afterlife: 10DS, a brainchild of the former advisor, is Downing Street's data science team, staffed by coders from start-ups and data visualisation specialists. Cummings takes immediate control of 10DS and moves them in beside where Yusuf's pick for the Policy Unit sit. As Downing Street is becoming an unlikely blend of data scientists and Reform faithfuls, Cummings turns his attention to Whitehall.

Most of Cummings' plans are more radical. In this scenario, he has completed a project he claimed to be working on in the summer of 2025: devising 'the Actual Plan' for what a new prime minister could do 'in the first hour, day, week, quarter, to set things on a profoundly different path'. In 2029, he still believes that 'a once-in-a-century burst of powerful, thoughtful energy' could transform a Whitehall which he believes has succeeded in concealing 'the reality of the PM's power' from the office holder. Just as Cummings has had time out in the wilds of Northumberland to think about what he would do if he was given a second chance, he's also had years to consider how the Civil Service might resist. In one memorable conversation with Farage in the weeks leading up to Reform's triumphant election, the prime minister had said, 'The blob will strike as soon as we make the slightest move.'

'Conflict works,' had been Cummings' reply.

In one of the first acts of his premiership, Farage asks Cummings to look into repealing the 2010 Constitutional Reform and Governance Act (CRAG), which creates the Civil Service in law. Cummings points out that with all the will in the world repealing the Act and replacing it with something new would take time to draft and implement. The principles of impartiality in the Civil Service go back much further than 2010 and can trace their roots to the Northcote-Trevelyan Report of 1854. For Reform's top team it was a lesson that not everything they hated started with Tony Blair. Yusuf hands the work to the new Policy Unit as their first challenge of government, while he works on a plan for a series of quick hits Farage can make on the 'blob' within days.

In the short term, Farage could copy Cummings' former boss and appoint a First Civil Service Commissioner who was 'one of us'. Johnson had appointed Baroness Gisela Stuart, the former Vote Leave chair, into the role in 2022. But forcing out Stuart may not be necessary, given that during the Brexit referendum she showed she could work closely with Farage. Another immediate weapon Farage has in his attack on Whitehall is his role as Minister for the Civil Service: he ultimately has legal oversight into appointments and issuing a Code of Conduct, which he must do on becoming prime minister. If he has the support of the Commissioner, Farage is able to begin unofficially blocking appointments of civil servants to senior positions whom he thinks won't toe the line. This just leaves those that are already in post to deal with: as was shown when Truss got rid of Tom Scholar, the permanent secretary at the Treasury, days into her premiership, in the end if a prime minister wants to get rid of people, they can. They may have to pay significant compensation, but undesirable officials at the most senior levels can be dispatched with or without CRAG.

In the longer term, when the act is repealed, Cummings has free range to 'bring in the brightest and best from around the private sector into the Civil Service', according to a statement released to the lobby. Farage introduces Britain's first political cabinet secretary, a pliant former permanent secretary whose family has given generously to the Party ahead of the election. Cummings had identified her while working for Johnson as someone politically aligned with Reform. Unofficial politicisation of Civil Service roles is hardly new: when Tony Blair came into power, he brought in Jonathan Powell as his chief of staff, who went on to effectively replace the role of principal private secretary, the most important official who works in Downing Street every day.[14] Farage's new cabinet secretary agrees to ignore the Cabinet Manual and the Nolan Principles (which are Selflessness, Integrity, Objectivity, Accountability, Openness, Honesty and Leadership), a set of standards for those holding public office. Every PM is given the opportunity to write their own Ministerial Code, which usually says ministers have to listen to advice from officials: Farage simply scraps it. It is easy; neither of these are written into law.

In fact, many changes to the British system can happen at speed given the state's constitutional arrangements and political will from a radical new government. Theoretically, there is almost nothing which cannot be changed by Downing Street through orders from the prime minister or, if required, Acts of Parliament. Even if it takes a little bit of time. This does not mean there will

---

[14] There was still a PPS in place, but Powell and Alastair Campbell were given managerial powers through an Order in Council.

not be considerable opposition to Farage and Cummings' plans, but they are keen to push to the absolute limits the great deal of power the prime minister enjoys over the British state, something Starmer in 2025 had been criticised for not grasping. In 2029, the pair are determined to not make the same mistake.

The repeal of CRAG allows Farage to begin the process of ripping apart the independent Civil Service across its hundreds of thousands of employees. The quickest way to start would be to remove the need for 'Objectivity' and 'Impartiality' within the Civil Service Code. Meanwhile, Cummings strengthens the role of special advisors and gives them powers to directly manage career civil servants, including permanent secretaries. For many career Mandarins, this is the final straw.

In protest at the proposed changes, hundreds of senior civil servants resign and these positions are quickly filled by the heads of Tufton Street think-tanks, business leaders and former Reform advisors. Eventually, contracts for civil servants are introduced, which can be easily terminated based on performance. But officials suspect the reviews will be informed by their suspected political allegiance. It is the beginning of the end of the permanent Civil Service after almost 200 years. Management consultants flood into departments to replace those on strike – they confidently promise to find billions of pounds in efficiencies. Farage has little interest in the detail of Whitehall so he is more than happy to officially delegate his powers over the Service to Cummings.

There is outrage from senior civil servants in the First Division Association union, but a public battle with an unsympathetic union would likely benefit Farage. A clearout of Whitehall is exactly what Reform has always wanted: Sarah Pochin, the MP for Runcorn and Helsby, takes the cameras with her as she goes on a tour of Whitehall with a clipboard, earmarking empty office space, submitting applications to end the leases of department buildings. In the end, there are fewer resignations across the board than many had predicted: civil servants decide, in a period of intense job market uncertainty, that they may struggle to find similar well-paid employment in the private sector. Regardless, they steel themselves for what lies ahead with the knowledge that they serve the elected government and the British people have chosen Reform. It is their duty to try to keep things on the right lines.

In comparison, other 'machinery of government' changes to Whitehall departments are easier, and follow reorganisations which often happen following a change of administration. In Farage's first week, the Ministry of Defence is renamed the War Office[15] and 'Net Zero' is junked from Ed Miliband's former department's name. The Department for Environment, Food & Rural Affairs becomes the Department for Water and Food Security. All the changes, which are set in motion on the first day but unfold over months, are designed to shift power into the hands of Farage and in his inner circle: Cummings knew they would need the levers of government to comply if they were going to implement his designs for Britain.

That night, the paint is drying on new signs outside Whitehall departments, and officials who refuse to put those plans in place gather with their cardboard boxes at Westminster's pubs to drown their sorrows. They know that with the support of the press and the glow from his election win, Farage's poll ratings will soar. Before he turns in for his first night in Downing Street, Farage instructs his staff to begin the introduction of the Great Repeal Bill to the Commons.

---

[15] Its name from 1857 to 1964.

3

Deportation Nation

Eleven Days After Election Night

Monday, 9 July 2029, 10.45 a.m.

The prime minister's private secretary requests an urgent meeting about the 'situation in Calais'. Nigel Farage's announcement on the steps of Downing Street that his government will immediately legislate for a Great Repeal Bill (GRB) has led to hundreds more attempted crossings on the Channel. Border Force is close to being overwhelmed, his private secretary warns, and the Royal National Lifeboat Institution (RNLI) is mounting its largest ever campaign to help those in peril at sea. The week previously, 12 people drowned after their boat capsized. The body of a child had washed up on Dunkirk beach. The picture appears on front pages globally and symbolises the crisis. Farage has been silent.

Farage's foreign policy private secretary joins the meeting and describes the geopolitical reasons for the spike. Asylum seekers are fleeing an eruption of conflict in the Middle East. Hundreds of thousands of terrified people are desperately trying to reach safe countries in the surrounding region, or beginning on the perilous journey to what they hope will be safety in Europe.

The Continent is plunged into a second migration crisis, with scenes not witnessed since 2015 being played out on its border. This time, migration policies are far stricter and those seeking sanctuary from state violence often find themselves repelled with military force. But some manage to make it into the EU against all odds and some travel to northern France.

When Farage stood at the lectern and announced Britain was leaving the ECHR, repealing the Human Rights Act and disapplying the Refugee Convention, all in one piece of legislation, the numbers surged and people smugglers began to charge extra. No one wanted to be repelled by a Navy vessel. The news carried pictures of thousands of Syrian men forced into giant warehouses with no sanitation or assistance from the French government, who are also staging a crackdown. The crisis in the Channel had reached a terrifying climax. Among the beneficiaries is the Reform Party, who plan to use the increase in numbers as political coverage for their new Bill. They know they are in for a battle in both chambers, and with the EU. But by 2029 Hungary is also set on leaving the ECHR, so Farage believes he has some short-term cover as Brussels will have to tread carefully. After Zia Yusuf's surprise failure to win a seat, the man Farage turns to is Ashfield's Lee Anderson, Britain's new home secretary.

Wednesday, 25 July 2029, 1.15 p.m.

'Nothing like the Great British curry house,' Anderson says as the waiter pulls out the chair for him at Gandhi's, Westminster. The home secretary is having dinner with a Reform donor who has helped fund his campaign in Ashfield – he was someone the secretary of state could talk to in the full knowledge it wouldn't end up on the front page of a broadsheet the next day. The restaurant too had been selected for privacy: they could have gone to the

Cinnamon Club on Great Smith Street, but the risk of running into Peston or Gove was too great. Gandhi's, with its butter chicken special and pints of Kingfisher, was all he needed to fuel his rants about the department and fellow Cabinet members.

When he thought back nearly a month ago to his first day on the job, it had hardly lived up to expectations. Government sources in 2025 complained that the Home Office did not feel much like a 'Great Office of State'. 'You've got boarded-up windows so that people can't shoot the home secretary in her office, so it's all quite dark,' said one, 'and it's impossible to see outside.' 'We don't get any sunlight. Why do you think we're all so miserable?' they joked. While the secretary of state's office is dark, the rest of Marsham Street is modern and bright. Even by its standards, there was an atmosphere of dejection on the arrival of the former Reform chief whip in the department. 'It's so dark, it's like being down the bloody mines again,' Anderson, a former National Union of Mineworkers member, jokes about his new office, before ordering a round of poppadoms.

'I look around and I think, I'm in the shit. Danny gets to swan around in the Foreign Office doing absolutely nothing, Ticey will do tax cuts eventually and get all the credit, and I'm going to be called a Nazi for deporting some foreign chancers,' he moans as he dives a spoon into a dish of chutney.

With arrivals increasing every day, Anderson and his advisors were under pressure to find immediate answers. A bill of the size of the GRB would take up to a year to pass and then there was the delicate process and nuances of the Commons and Lords to navigate. Process and nuance were not something that came naturally to Anderson: he needs a quick win.

'I got one of my advisors to call James Orr up and bring him and his lads from the Research Department down. Brain the size of a planet, that guy. You should have seen the perm sec's face. But he led the department access talks so I thought it was worth getting him involved,' he says. In 2025, Orr was a regular presence in the front row of Reform press conferences, although he had yet to take a full public role in policy presentation. But he was revered in the Party for bringing intellectual weight to their plans. In this scenario, it was Orr to whom Farage had turned on election night to hand him the brown file containing their plans for the Great Repeal Bill, and Anderson needed him to make sense of what was to come. Needless to say, the permanent secretary wasn't happy about it.

'I remember your perm sec from school,' the donor says, looking around for the waiter to request lime pickle. 'Missed out on being head boy because the headmaster decided he couldn't command the confidence of the rugby team.'

The waiter arrives with two pints: 'What will it be this evening, sir?'

After ordering, the donor asks how the 'deportations stuff' is coming along. Anderson wants to slam his head on the table in frustration. As well as repealing the Human Rights Act, leaving the ECHR and disapplying the Refugee Convention, Reform advisors explained to officials that within the same bill they wanted to dramatically expand deportations. As Donald Trump had done in his Big Beautiful Bill in 2025 on government spending, Farage told Anderson he wanted to capitalise on their political honeymoon and front-load the radical changes at the start of the Parliament so by 2034 he could point to his success. 'We may not get this same opportunity again, Lee. We've waited so long for this and we've got one shot. Who knows how long we can keep this lot in line?' Farage said as he appointed Anderson in the Cabinet Room the day following the election. The home secretary barely knew where to begin.

The donor brought Reform's manifesto up on his phone to remind himself of what the Party had promised before the election. This was important because under the Salisbury Convention, peers in the Lords are not meant to block manifesto commitments. The manifesto proposed introducing a statutory duty for the home secretary to deport illegal migrants; to disapply legal protections for migrants so they could not use them to delay their deportation; strengthening detention powers to detain someone indefinitely and mandatory criminal sanctions for anyone who destroyed their ID before arriving in the UK, a practice common among those arriving on small boats. The Bill would also set up a new 'UK Deportation Command', integrating the Home Office's data systems with police, the NHS, HMRC, DVLA and banks to identify and deport a target of 600,000 people. The Party promised before the election to boost detention capacity to 24,000 people within 18 months. Migrants would be removed on five flights a day from airports near detention centres. The manifesto said the policies would cost £10 billion over five years, but there would be a saving of £7 billion in the first five years and £42 billion over a decade due to lower benefits claims and accommodation. He put away his phone as Anderson returned from the loo.

The waiter excused himself as he laid hot plates on the table for their mains, while presenting colourful dishes of tandoori chicken skewers and onion bhajis in front of them.

'It's a flagship policy, so it'll be first on the PM's priority list, but getting it through both Houses is going to be a bloody nightmare. In a way, they had it lucky during Covid: they had a crisis and at least at the start, most thought they had to get on with it. We're being fucked on the border right now and I still have to pay attention to what a court in Strasbourg thinks, even though we're demanding to get out of it. The British Bill of Rights is another headache: we can't repeal the Human Rights Act before we get that sorted. I have no idea how much time it will all take, we need a quick win.'

In the Home Office, Anderson is already facing opposition from officials being forced to work with Orr's political team. A government source predicts that the reality of the operational challenges would immediately puncture Reform's grand ambitions for hundreds of thousands of deportations. 'The operational capacity is just not going to be there for years,' they said. 'You don't have the detention space and they say they're going to have five flights a day: well, they need to get a service provider to do those flights and that'll take months to find someone.' They pointed out that Reform would have to negotiate private sector contracts with companies like Serco to ramp up removals, which was likely to take months and cost hundreds of millions more. 'The same goes for deportation flights. It's not a military flight that does it, it's an actual airline, so you then have to work out the relationship with the commercial airline and the private contractors to move these people around the country.'

As plates of butter chicken and Goan fish curry arrive in front of them accompanied not long after by a sizzling dish of spicy lamb chops, Anderson explains that part of the issue is that no one told him Labour were already been doing loads of 'ICE-style' raids: Border Force was at capacity just targeting barber shops, car wash businesses and nail salons, let alone expanding beyond businesses and targeting illegal migrants at home. 'I was delighted when Tice agreed funding for Border Force. The next day, I learn it will take up to a year to hire more officers. One of the officials said to me: "Minister, if we're bending over backwards to hire police officers, why would they choose to become an immigration enforcement officer? We'll need to pay them double."' After hours of meetings with his private office, Anderson had become sick of hearing their objections and ordered the most disputatious officials be moved on.

'I need something I can point to in the next month to say: yes, we're up shit creek but at least this department is good for something. What were we thinking? Of course we weren't going to get five flights a day, returns deals and ICE-style roundups in the first eighteen months. Madness. I blame Zia and his podcast interviews.'

'This is what the blob does to every minister. If you are weak, they will control you,' the donor said, his mouth stuffed with naan. 'You've been captured by that bed-wetting permanent secretary, Lee. I was listening to a podcast with Steve Bannon recently: he said Reform must "flood the zone" after the election. Do what Donald did. Week one after the inauguration, Gulf of America; week two, tariffs on China, Mexico and Canada; week three, scrap all US overseas aid. The best comms hit in history. Listen, this government is spending billions on nonsense like these migrant hotels. Close them down – you're the big man, you're the secretary of state. You have the power to do it.'

As they are speaking, the two men scatter a meal's worth of sauce and rice across the thick white tablecloth. Their waiter returns with a table crumber and two hot white towels. He begins to clear away the empty pint glasses.

The donor turns to the waiter as he works. 'What do you think, mate? Should we chuck 'em all out on the street? Wouldn't get your lot's vote, would it?'

The waiter bites his tongue, finishes clearing, and finds his boss. By the time the manager has come back to tell the minister and donor never to visit Gandhi's again, they have stumbled off into the warm Westminster night.

Thursday, 26 July 2029, 9 a.m.

The home secretary, nursing a hangover, calls his most senior advisor and organises a meeting with his private office.

'Let's just scrap them. Just end them overnight, let them fend for themselves. I want you lot to immediately look into just ending the hotels – I'll chat with the boss and see what he thinks about it. This nonsense has gone on long enough.' There is silence from even the most ambitious of private secretaries: one government source said that the thinking within the department was that such a policy would almost double the homeless population in the country overnight. As of 2025, there were just over 100,000 asylum seekers in government paid-for accommodation, including 30,000 in hotels. As laws ban them from working, they would likely end up in the country's black market for labour, and tents sheltering them would appear on Britain's high streets. 'It would cause uproar, Minister. There is no proper documentation of them. Where do they go?' There would be anger at such a policy across Whitehall: the biggest reaction would likely be from the Ministry of Housing, Communities and Local Government, with significant and sudden pressure coming on social housing and sheltered accommodation. The regional mayors, who are on the frontline of dealing with homelessness, would also be in uproar.

When advisors in Downing Street during Rishi Sunak's tenure had discussed the idea, it was dismissed following predictions of huge encampments across the country, which would cost more in the long run due to a rise in mental health issues, criminality and disturbance. The officials eventually manage to talk Anderson down from closing all the hotels. In return, he exacts a commitment out of the department that they will immediately, despite capacity in the camps having yet to increase, ramp up removals, and begin shutting the most notorious accommodation sites.

'This is not going to end well,' his principal private secretary tells his deputy. Anderson leaves for the day feeling victorious, even though he'd had to threaten to push the nuclear button to have his way.

Wednesday, 22 August 2029, 2 p. m.

Lee Anderson is pleased to put the strife in the department behind him as he rises in the chamber on the debate on the second reading of the Great Repeal Bill. Farage has taken great pleasure in recalling Parliament from its long summer recess to begin passing what every MP knew was urgent legislation. The legislation was a flagship policy for Reform: candidates had been selected based on their support for the measures to ensure the Bill's safe passage through the Commons.

Or so Downing Street hoped. Anderson knows the GRB was beset on all sides by challenges. Despite having the numbers, Reform's whips warned that opposition MPs could try any number of tactics to disrupt its progress through last-ditch amendments, wrecking motions and delays. It was all on the table for a Bill as controversial as this. The BBC's new political editor on the broadcaster's *Newscast* podcast describes the mood of trepidation: 'Reform have done what no one said they could do: they have survived two months in Parliament. A Liz Truss government this is not – well, not yet, anyway. But now the Party has to govern and it has to show it is doing more than just taking on Whitehall. Farage will make immigration his administration's opening theme. In Lee Anderson, the Party has a bruiser who will approach Whitehall and Parliament with a sledgehammer. But all the most successful parties know how to play the game. A parliamentary oarsman who can navigate the treacherous shoals of Commons procedure, the home secretary is not. We have to remember what an aberration Reform is: the closest historical precedent is the first Labour government in 1924. But at that point Labour had been the main opposition party for two years, whereas Reform's MPs have been sidelined on the opposition benches for the last five years, much to Farage's annoyance. Labour in 1924 had Members of Parliament who understood how procedure worked. They were already baked into the process of the Commons. As the Great Repeal Bill begins to become a reality, Reform's parliamentary nous will be tested.'

'I commend this Bill to the House,' Anderson roars, to cheers from the government benches and slaps on the back from Farage and Tice.

The GRB must clear five steps in each House to become an act: first reading, second reading, committee stage, report stage, and third reading before the Commons and Lords settle the measures between themselves. The Bill then receives Royal Assent and becomes an Act of Parliament. At first reading, the title is read to the Commons and the full text is made public for the first time. At this stage, there is no vote on the Great Repeal Bill and it cannot be amended. Anderson is standing in the Commons at the second reading, where MPs have their first chance to debate the measures. Following him, shadow ministers and backbench MPs have an opportunity to make remarks.

Every Reform MP is in attendance: the men are wearing turquoise ties, the women in turquoise lapel pins. On the opposition benches, the Greens, Lib Dems and the SNP are all wearing badges of the black and orange Refugee Flag, which has become a common sight at protests against the GRB. At the dispatch box, Farage hails the legislation as the largest and most important change to domestic policy since the war. The Reform front bench taunts the opposition as the volume increases in the chamber and the new Speaker has to constantly pause the debate due to intemperate exchanges.

At the second reading, the Bill's principles are debated, but no amendments can be made. However, a member can propose a 'reasoned amendment' in opposition to the Bill in its entirety. There is outrage from the government benches when the Speaker – who is meant to be impartial but was chosen after Reform whips let it be known he was Farage's pick – selects Lib Dem Ed Davey's reasoned amendment to scrap the Bill. Farage thought this new Speaker would do his bidding, upending hundreds of years of parliamentary procedure and tradition. He had been wrong. The GRB would now have to clear an unexpectedly early parliamentary hurdle because of the actions of the Speaker.

While swearing support for the GRB was a prerequisite for MPs to be selected, recent history shows that a party can never be sure how ideologically consistent its MPs are: Starmer's Labour machine tried to rid the ranks of left-wing MPs, but many of the new intake voted against his benefits reforms in 2025. MPs see themselves as members of a party but also as representatives of their constituency. This means in practice no prime minister or home secretary, especially ones with as small a majority as Farage and Anderson, can rely fully on the work of their whips, whose job it is to keep Reform MPs in line.

Just weeks after the election, the new MPs that swell the ranks of the government benches hardly know each other and therefore there is little personal loyalty between them or to the front bench. Even though they might support the government, they might be perturbed at the flood of letters filling their inboxes from terrified constituents; they might be swayed by their husbands or wives, who have more of a capacity to lobby their opinion than any whip; or they might be cajoled by the arguments of lobbyists or campaign groups, who MPs often have connections with before their selection. All of those forces are weighing on the minds of the MPs as they sit in the chamber and watch

Davey's amendment be chosen. If they voted for it, the government's flagship policy would be ruined. It could bring down the whole administration.

Surely, they wouldn't dare?

Many MPs are angry at the appointment of a raft of business executives to the Lords so Farage can bring them into Cabinet. It was something the leader often spoke about during the campaign, but before the election they hadn't considered how it would affect their own chances of promotion: seeing a banker walk into the Treasury, who has no responsibilities to listen to his constituents in the endless Friday surgeries and can still enjoy the ministerial salary and a seat beside the prime minister in Cabinet, was galling to ambitious young Reform MPs. But in 2029, would this be enough to kill the Bill based on a proposal from the likes of Ed Davey? When the votes were read out, Farage, Anderson and the government had won and the Bill was to pass to the next stage.

The Speaker's treachery in the eyes of the prime minister is not forgotten. In Farage's parliamentary office, just behind the Speaker's chair, Farage rants about the duplicity of a man he put into his position of power. He commands Dan Jukes to get to work: intense online pressure comes on to the Speaker after historical claims emerge from employees of the company he used to run concerning workplace harassment. The Speaker is reported to the police over the allegations and suspended from office while he faces an investigation into the allegations. During that period, screen shots come to light which show him, while Speaker, 'liking' posts from Labour MPs which are critical of Farage on X. The prime minister tells his daily TikTok update that he has 'lost confidence' in the Speaker.[16] Giorgia Meloni has pioneered this comms strategy in Italy, regularly telling her followers on

---

[16] As of January 2026, Nigel Farage's personal accounts have 6.7 million followers across Facebook, X, Instagram and TikTok – more than any other UK politician.

the platform what she was doing for them and pointing the finger squarely at those who were holding progress back. Farage takes it one step further and makes it daily. This time, the PM points the finger squarely at the Speaker.

Despite his former colleagues writing an open letter defending the Speaker, the mud sticks and following the precedent set by Michael Marten, who resigned from the role over the expenses scandal in 2009, he leaves his office and is replaced by a vote in the House with a new Reform MP, this one more pliant than the last. Such tactics are not unfamiliar to those au fait with the dark arts of media manipulation: Reform's then head of policy Zia Yusuf reported ex-Reform MP Rupert Lowe for bullying in March 2025, an allegation Lowe said was vexatious and brought against him because he spoke out against Farage. Former staff members described the idea Lowe was a bully as 'nonsense' and the Crown Prosecution Service (CPS) dropped its case. When relationships sour in the Party, things can turn very nasty. After the ejection of the Speaker, Farage could be satisfied there would be no more surprises in the Commons.

The Bill now passes to the committee stage, the longest part of its passage. The make-up of parliamentary committees reflects the share of MPs a party has in the House, so the government has the advantage. This means it seldom loses a vote here. The Great Repeal Bill is of such a scale that by procedure it has to be taken into consideration by the whole House, meaning all MPs have the opportunity to discuss the proposals in the chamber. This slows down the progress of the Bill considerably, as instead of discussion among a small group of MPs in a committee room, weeks of parliamentary time has to be allocated for potentially hundreds of representatives to have their say.

This is where Reform's ability to reach out and talk to opposition parties is tested: in the process of getting a complicated Bill through Parliament, normally the government works with opposition parties to help smooth proceedings. This might come as a surprise to anyone who has watched the theatrics at Prime Minister's Questions, but even with a big majority, other parties are considered. For example, at the committee stage the government will agree through the 'usual channels', meaning with opposition whips, how long a debate should go on for. 'A lot of it is done on gentlemanly terms behind the scenes,' said one parliamentary expert. 'If that has broken down, then you are in uncharted territory and it is not a place where things will happen quickly or easily.'

In 2029, Reform whips have a general disdain for the likes of the caretaker Labour leader, Peter Kyle, and Ed Davey, let alone Green Party leader Zack Polanski and the SNP's Stephen Flynn. As they are able to command a majority, the government ultimately controls the agenda, so even without the consent of opposition parties they can press on: however, this leaves the Bill vulnerable to wrecking amendments and opposition MPs trying to take control of the order paper to try and pass their own agenda. The breakdown in the Commons will produce a situation in which there are forces at work to obstruct it and water it down.

But Labour, His Majesty's official opposition in 2029, are in disarray following their election defeat. Kyle, Leader of the Opposition, has decided to whip his MPs into abstaining on the measures. He doesn't want his party to seem out of touch with the clear anti-immigration message sent by voters at the election. Labour are no stranger to seemingly bizarre policy positions following an election defeat. In 2015, caretaker leader Harriet Harman whipped MPs to abstain on the Tory government's welfare cuts. In 2029, the soft left of 50 MPs defy the whip and vote against. Kyle is encouraged by the majority of the Party, which has swung firmly to the right. He proposes they vote for an amendment to the Bill which sets out their objections, but the left of the Party are implacably opposed and Labour's infighting becomes the story.

Zack Polanski is delighted as the Greens set out with members of the SNP and the Liberal Democrats to form an opposition block to Reform's proposals.

'If this bill goes through, the sight of our neighbours being rounded up in the street by unmarked vehicles will become commonplace in communities up and down this country,' one Green MP warns in a debate.

'This debate extends far beyond the plight of small boats, migrants and asylum seekers. The motion put forward today affects every single one of us. The Prime Minister is coming not for the human rights of the migrant, but the human rights of every British citizen,' a Lib Dem MP adds.

At the vote at the Committee stage, the 'usual channels' have broken down and the members of opposition parties are seen trotting up and down College Green with copies of *Erskine May*, the parliamentary handbook on procedure, tucked underneath their arms. They introduce amendments to force votes and test Reform MPs for weakness, which requires extra time to debate the new proposals. They call emergency debates on procedural issues and grab any Reform MP who will talk to them in the tearooms and whisper in their ears about the threat the bill poses to liberty, democracy and free speech. Most are left cold and shuffle off to the Strangers' Bar. Undeterred, the Greens and the Liberal Democrats organise a mass campaign to encourage their supporters in Reform constituencies to write to their MPs. Such is the confusion caused in the ranks of new Reform MPs that one representative from Norfolk stands up from the government benches in a committee debate and speaks at length about his disgust at the Bill, after being alerted to it by his constituents. He has to be told quietly by colleagues that he is meant to be supporting the motion and he quickly gives way, with the rest of the House descending into peals of laughter.

That latest episode, and the general slow progress of legislation through the lower house, is deeply frustrating to the new prime minister. He realises he must do more than haul the chief whip in for a dressing down. He knew the legislation would be difficult to get through the Commons, but he thought with a majority he would be able to make the political weather. Instead, he is stuck in endless rounds of ludicrous debates, while 'illegal migrants' continue to arrive on the South Coast. A snap poll at the start of October puts his ratings at the lowest they have been since before his sudden rise in 2025. If the election was held today, the *Daily Mail* front page runs, Reform would be dozens of seats off a majority. Were his supporters on Fleet Street about to turn on him? Farage is looking ahead to a clash with the Lords. He sends a WhatsApp message to his closest allies – Jukes, Banks, Cottrell – to meet in his office when he is back from Parliament. They are going to have to think big.

Friday, 12 October 2029, 10 a.m.

As he arrives outside the Bell Inn Hotel, outside Epping to the north-east of London, the home secretary smiles when he sees what Reform's events team has created. A turquoise marquee stands outside the migrant hotel, which had become the scene of protests in summer of 2025 after one occupant, Hadush Gerberslasie Kebatu, was charged with sexually assaulting a 14-year-old girl. Local residents and members of the far right descended on it, and it wasn't long before Kemi Badenoch and the then Tory justice secretary Robert Jenrick were there too. Anderson is impressed by the spread the team has laid on: it's a beautiful day, and the plates of bacon rolls and tea in blue and white china cups are delightful. Pachelbel's Canon is playing on speakers as the press pack arrives.

The migrant hotel is a symbol of Labour's inability to tackle migration: the owners had expanded it over the years to meet the increasing demand and had cut costs on heating and maintenance. The paint on the mock Tudor exterior is peeling and a high barbed-wire fence had been erected around the exterior to keep protesters out. There are bars on the windows. But today, Anderson is to announce that Reform, after so many years, is finally closing the Bell Inn. It was another Reform victory, he tells Peston, GB News' Christopher Hope and the *Spectator*'s Tim Shipman as he works the marquee. 'My officials said it couldn't be done,' he says. 'You've just got to know when to put your foot down.'

10.30 a.m.

Standing on stage, the home secretary is almost palpating with excitement as he begins his speech: 'In 1997, we knew who we were. The population was stable. Immigration was under control. Then we had 30 years of unprecedented illegal migration. I want to send a message to all 1.2 million illegal immigrants who have come here without permission. We will detain you and then deport you. We are going to deport, deport, deport. You're not going to end up in a cosy three-star hotel like the one behind me. No. You'll be detained in one of our expanded detention centres which Reform is pumping funding into. This will mean we can do much more of what we're doing today, bringing these hotels to an orderly close. They have been a terrible stain on our national culture.'

The number 1.2 million had been discussed by the Party since they first went mainstream in the summer of 2025.

When party chairman Zia Yusuf was challenged on it on the right-wing podcast *Triggernometry* in June 2025, he said Reform would 'direct every instrument of state' to deport over a million people, even if it took dragging men and women who had been in the UK since they were children from their homes. 'We're going to do it in a way which prioritises the rule of law. But yes, to be direct about it, yes, if you are here illegally, I think that does need to be done. British people expect it and I think there is popular support for that,' he told the hosts. The figure is based on work done by the Pew Research Center think-tank in 2019, which said in 2017 between 800,000 to 1.2 million unauthorised immigrants were resident in the UK. But the organisation has since admitted failings in its methodology and admitted the estimate was flawed. In 2025, while Reform vowed to deport 600,000 over five years if elected, this did not stop its leaders from repeating the higher figures multiple times publicly.

But the reporters have heard all this before. The speech was for the cameras: the news lines would come in the questions afterwards. The BBC's political editor was eventually chosen to speak: 'Home Secretary, we have seen official warnings from inside your department that this policy of closing down hotels and transferring more migrants to Manston is going to cause overcrowding at the facility and that the tented accommodation you're providing there isn't fit for habitation. We've also seen internal documents from MHCLG [the Ministry of Housing, Communities, and Local Government] which say the policy has the potential to cause disorder on high streets if the new camps are not secure. Are you putting public order at risk, Home Secretary?' The assembled audience began to grumble and boo as the political editor finished speaking.

'Project Fear is making a comeback again at the BBC, I see! We are not closing down all migrant hotels. No one wants to see 30,000 fighting-age men roaming high streets. But look, as we ramp up capacity with extra funding for Border Force, it's only right that we end the scourge of these hotels on our communities. I'm proud that we will divert funds from our Civil Service cuts to shore up the men and women who are on the front line of the illegal immigration crisis at our border, but also in our towns and cities.'

In December 2025, Danny Kruger, the Party's then lead on preparation for government, pledged to cut 70,000 roles from the Civil Service, while protecting the jobs of those working at the Border Force. 'As the Great Repeal Bill makes its way through Parliament, this is meant as a reminder to the people who voted for us that a Reform government is on your side.'

Friday, 19 October 2029, 6 a.m.

At the Manston arrivals and processing centre, things have not been this bad since the autumn of 2022. The former military base is hidden by high trees three miles inland from Ramsgate, Kent, and is run by the outsourcing company Mitie on behalf of the state. It was opened in 2022 in response to the surge in small boat crossings, and has been the venue for a litany of human rights abuses and violent disturbances since. Manston has the capacity for 1,600 people to stay for a short period, but in the autumn of 2022, it held 4,000 people. Detainees slept on the floor or on cardboard and there were outbreaks of diphtheria and scabies. The facility is meant to be a processing site where people are kept for only 24 hours, before they are either sent to migrant hotels or an immigration detention centre if the UK government believes it has a case to remove them. During the summer and autumn of 2022, some 18,000 people out of a total of 29,000 were detained there beyond the 24-hour limit. The longest someone was detained was 32 days. In 2023, the then immigration minister Robert Jenrick was criticised for ordering that a mural in the family marquee at Manston which had been praised by inspectors be painted over. In 2025, it was the subject of an ongoing public inquiry.

By 2029, the inquiry has published a damning report, but the site is still in use and has been selected for expansion by the Reform government as part of its manifesto pledge to increase capacity to 24,000 spaces. As one of the largest facilities in the system, Lee Anderson chooses Manston to take the asylum seekers formerly housed at the Bell Inn, as well as those accommodated at seven other hotels he is keen to close down. The asylum seekers are meant to be there for processing before removals, but as in 2022, that process has broken down entirely following the surge in new crossings.

The coaches arrive at the gates and the passengers are taken to processing gazebos erected outside the site's main building. They are carrying what few possessions they have – a bag of clothes, puffer jackets, a file of documents. The new detainees at Manston are mostly young men, but among their number are families and young women with babies too. The head of operations at Manston begs the home secretary on the phone to pause the transfer, but the home secretary refuses, citing the extra funding he had just been given. Before their arrival, dozens of new tents are hastily erected on the little land left available for expansion.

Manston was to become Anderson's quick win.

11.15 a.m.

At Manston, three men – all civil engineers by training – are told that they are being transferred to a detention centre, from where they will be put on a flight and deported to

Syria as they entered Britain illegally. As it had been in 2026, Syria is a country from where asylum applications are increasing, as well as Eritrea, Vietnam, Pakistan and Bangladesh. Room has to be made for the new arrivals. There is no one else available, so a 19-year-old custody officer is selected to drive the three through Ramsgate town in a secure van. In 2029, Mitie company policy is that guards never go on their own on these drives, but Manston has endemic staffing issues due to the conditions at the centre and the low pay. It's no one's first choice of employment. When the driver stops on the side of the road into town to take a call from his pregnant girlfriend, the men realise they have a chance to escape. If they are taken back to Syria, their lives will be in danger and everything they sacrificed to find asylum will have been for nothing: they are terrified. Together, they ram at the door, which was not properly secured, and manage to burst it open. The driver, who has taken the opportunity to relieve himself by the side of the road after his call, has barely time to zip up his trousers before two of the men run towards the town, with the other heading in the opposite direction.

Such errors have happened before as part of operations at Manston: in November 2022, 11 asylum seekers were abandoned at London Victoria station without accommodation or warm clothing after being moved out to avoid overcrowding. A homelessness charity who helped them said they were 'stressed' and 'disturbed' as they struggled to work out what to do. The pair who head to Ramsgate feel the same way. They spend the next hour wandering around the town, carrying their possessions and buying a packet of cigarettes and a wrap for lunch, with their combined £9.95 per week allowance. But it is not too long before an elderly man spots them looking at phones in a shop window and calls the police. By the time the police arrive, a gang of teenagers have started hurling abuse at the pair and a fight has broken out. People are filming the scene as someone's dog attacks one of the Syrian refugees. It takes officers half an hour to break up the fight and arrest the pair and take them back to Manston. The clips begin to circulate on TikTok and it is not long before they are picked up by the national media.

Faris, the third man, ran because that was what the others had told him to do. He thought they were behind him until he had stopped and looked. As he wanders the flat landscape of fields, he becomes confused. A psychologist had recently assessed him as suffering from severe post-traumatic stress disorder: he had lost his wife and only daughter during a missile attack in Damascus following hostilities between the government and rebels, and had followed his two closest friends all the way to Ramsgate.

As Faris gets lost in the streets after dark that night, a car pulls up beside him.

'You alright, dear?'

'Can you take me?'

'Yes, where to?'

'Manston, please.'

'Are you sure?'

'Yes, it's cold. I want to go to Manston, please.'

'My name is Bernadette,' the woman says. She has a rosary hung around her rear-view mirror – Manston was on the way home from church. 'Hop in.'

Tuesday, 15 January 2030, 6 p.m.

Back in Downing Street, Farage is becoming increasingly concerned about reports that despite efforts to appease his backbenchers by tearing into the BBC, his majority for the Great Repeal Bill is slipping away once more. The Opposition's actions to slow down the course of the Bill and to lean on his pliable new Reform MPs are beginning to work. That evening, reports emerge of the largest-ever single day of migrant crossings in the Channel.

'That's it, get Dom in here,' he tells his diary manager. Cummings had recommended he call a COBR (Cabinet Office Briefing Rooms) meeting to demonstrate he was taking a grip on the situation in the Channel – in parlance of the Labour government of 2025, these are referred to as SHOWBRs rather than COBRs, as they are intended for 'show' rather than for any actual decision making. COBR is a Cabinet committee which meets during moments of national crisis or emergency and convenes all the major relevant parties during such an event.

A snap poll shows a ratings bump for Farage following the move and he tells GB News viewers there is only one solution to the crisis in the Channel: send in the Navy. The call to send in the military has long been made by those on the right and one of its most vocal supporters is Farage's now senior advisor, Dominic Cummings. In June 2025, Cummings told the *Telegraph* that 'operationally, it's obviously simple to stop the boats. You can deploy the Navy, you can stop the boats.' He said the 'entire problem' was Britain's adherence to the ECHR and the Human Rights Act. 'It is not possible for the British prime minister now to deploy the Navy and do the things that you need to do in order to stop the boats. The courts will declare it unlawful because of the Human Rights Act so you have to repeal the Human Rights Act. You have to state that you are withdrawing from the jurisdiction of the Strasbourg Court [the ECHR], you deploy the Navy and stop the boats and you say nobody is landing from these boats.' Cummings advocated for the boats to be 'destroyed' and the people smugglers to be put on the Special Forces' 'kill or capture' list.

That night, Nigel Farage goes on GB News to tell his MPs: vote for my Bill or you will be blamed by the public for preventing me from taking the requisite action to save Britain.

Meanwhile, the head of operations at Manston calls the chief constable at Kent Police to warn of a spate of recent disturbances at the facility, after an internal rapid review of the facility following the escapes had landed on his desk. 'There'll be a riot here one day, believe me,' he says. With the influx of new arrivals following the closure of the handful of migrant hotels, conditions had deteriorated: toilets were overflowing and staff were refusing to come into work. Overnight, a section of one of the tents had collapsed and on-site doctors had reported a rise in cases in diphtheria once more. All these presented challenges, but the thing that concerned him the most was the possibility of widespread disorder, and the risk of someone getting killed.

Wednesday, 16 January 2030, 9 a.m.

The following day, a *Times* investigation is published into the conditions at Manston: it alleges that the place was overrun with rats, that overcrowding had made fights and thefts common and that detainees had been kicked and beaten by guard staff. There are also allegations that drugs are being offered to detainees by members of staff, including to mothers in the crèche looking after young children.[17] The head of operations launches an inquiry into the accusations.

The story, which runs on the front page, takes only the second slot on the cover. 'Great Repeal Bill Clears Commons in Victory for Farage,' is the main headline. Alongside is a picture of the jubilant home secretary throwing caps with

---

[17] Such behaviour was reported at Manston in 2022 and contracted staff were disciplined.

'I ❤ GRB' on them, accompanied by the Union Jack flag, to a crowd at College Green outside the Palace of Westminster.

'Bill Set for Showdown in the Lords,' the standfirst reads.

Sunday, 20 January 2030, 11 a.m.

Earlier that morning, the Labour leader of the House of Lords was on *Sunday* with Chris Mason. The former political editor was quizzing the peer over the Salisbury Convention, the parliamentary custom that said the Lords would never delay a manifesto commitment. As the measures laid out in the Great Repeal Bill – leaving the European Convention on Human Rights, repealing the Human Rights Act, disapplying the Refugee Conventions, a new British Bill of Rights, as well as a host of detention proposals – were openly discussed by the Party before 2029, the obscure Salisbury Convention has suddenly become an important item of debate. Will the Lords break with precedent and defy the Prime Minister? In 2025, Farage said at a press conference his party were already thinking about the Convention, hinting that he considered a tussle with the Lords likely.

'Because of the decisions of the previous government, Labour now have a majority in the House of Lords. Surely you will use your power to delay this legislation as much as you can, given the general dislike for the measures in the upper house?'

'Peers will do all they can – as they always do – to scrutinise legislation, to make it the best it can be,' the peer said.

'So, is that a yes to my question? You will block it?'

'Chris, as I've said, the legislation has been passed to us now, we will look at it and suggest changes if the Bill requires it.'

It is not hard for the political editors of Sunday newspapers to call the Labour grandee to check what they think he is hinting: unelected peers are willing to use their powers to block the legislation for up to a year. Farage summons a meeting of his top advisors in Downing Street: it is inconceivable that his Bill will be held up by this fool. What can be done? he asks his team.

Being unelected, the Lords are without a democratic mandate: they are officially the backstop to the Commons, but in reality, lack the democratic legitimacy to be a fully effective challenge to the lower house. Even though the Commons has power over the Lords, peers can still make life very difficult for Farage. The Salisbury Convention is just that – a convention, and can easily be ignored. Once the Bill is voted on by the Commons at the Third Reading, it then goes to the Lords, where it is debated and amended before a process known as 'ping pong' where both Houses resolve their differences over amendments. In the prime minister's office, the colour drains from his face as it is explained to him that the Great Repeal Bill (GRB), his flagship legislation which he needs to pass before he can begin to show the electorate results, could take many years to come into effect.

So, what can Reform do to clip the Lords' wings? As in 1911 when the Commons and Lords clashed over Lloyd George's budget, couldn't the Commons pass a motion to significantly reduce their powers and force them to accept? Again, Farage was advised, it would take over a year for the legislation to pass, although they could try and threaten the peers with it to see how they'd react. Even then, this would have to pass the upper house. What about stuffing the Lords with his own selections, one of his advisors suggests, and offers to begin drawing up a list of possible Reform peers.[18]

---

[18] Farage could even threaten to hold a referendum on the existence of an unelected upper chamber. But it would likely be an empty threat in the short term due to the expense and time constraints of holding such a vote.

While they consider their options, Farage orders Dan Jukes and his team of pirates to launch a campaign to bombard the troublesome peers. The *Daily Mail* reheats its infamous headline: 'More Traitors of the People,' it rants with pictures of 12 Lords that have spoken out against Reform's plans. Reporters are handed protected 'off-diary' time to delve into the backgrounds of peers who have defended human rights cases in the past but these are only the most traditional and visible tactics used by those wishing to pressurise members of the upper house. The websites of multiple Lords are hacked, with people clicking on their links redirected to a spurious list claiming to name all the migrant sex offenders in the country. An anonymous campaign to flood social media with deepfakes (videos that have been manipulated so that the subject looks like someone else) somehow goes mainstream. The anonymous accounts behind the Yookay community on X start sharing the videos alongside phone-snatchings and vandalised tube carriages. There are even reports that Russia has jumped on the trend and is using bot farms in Siberia to create huge engagement for the posts.

Online agitators scour the internet for any trace of peers criticising Farage, Reform or the GRB: whenever they post online, they receive hundreds of death threats and abusive comments. Records of migrant charities they have supported in the past are sent to right-wing journalists.

In a meeting in California, the entrepreneur Elon Musk orders a push notification to a post from far-right activist Tommy Robinson containing a screenshot of messages exchanged between a peer and a migrant claimant, in which he called Farage a fascist. It is only later revealed that the screenshot was faked, but by then it has already been seen 15 million times.

Tommy Robinson, whose real name is Stephen Christopher Yaxley-Lennon, becomes a leading figure in the witch-hunt.

But whereas once he would have been outside the Lords in the cold with a friend filming him accosting peers, in 2029 Robinson has gone mainstream. He started with appearances on right-wing podcasts such as Harrison Pitt's *Deprogrammed* and Laurie Wastell's *The Sceptic*. There, he discussed his childhood in Luton, his two black Labradors, his mental health, his advice for Farage on where to go next with the GRB. He appears plugged in, a John the Baptist to Farage's Messiah.

Soon, the nationals come knocking and Robinson is pictured in the *Sunday Telegraph* with his dogs, talking about his battle to overcome the trauma following his imprisonment in 2024. He's far from a national treasure, but he goes from pariah status to hosting a successful podcast with a mainstream production company and sets up a men's mental health charity. In one episode, he makes a knowing reference to 'the terrible people who were responsible for giving this government all their ideas' – 'Some of them, shamelessly, are trying to reinvent themselves as podcasters,' he jokes. After years of being denied spots on political panel discussions, Robinson is invited on to the BBC's *Question Time* to discuss the government, the passage of the GRB and the clash with the Lords. He receives applause from a significant minority of the Home Counties audience when he says the Lords should be packed with Reform peers who will 'take our country back'.

'This is an issue of national security. Do you really trust these unelected Labour peers to do anything about the crisis in the channel? They are a national embarrassment,' he declares.

These days, Robinson is winning twice: he stands independent of the governing party as they teeter on the edge of oblivion, while seeing them attempt to enact the policy platform he's been advocating for years.

11.10 a.m.

Meanwhile, at Manston, four detainees have begun a hunger strike in protest against the conditions faced by the refugees. Seven thousand people are being kept on the site which until recently had capacity for less than a quarter of that number. Many are housed in long white marquees with flimsy metal fences around the perimeter. Some of them have been at the site for over a month: personal smartphones are removed from people when they arrive on site, but a few have managed to smuggle them inside so they can continue to contact family. Those without the means to contact their loved ones on the outside are becoming desperate and restless.

In support of the hunger strikers, the Our Rights radical action group, which has swelled in size over the months since the election, march from Ramsgate train station to the disused Manston airfield. The organisers were shocked at the response when Zack Polanski, the popular leader of the Green Party, asked a question which mentioned the demonstration at Prime Minister's Questions the week before. Two hundred thousand people watch the group's TikTok, sharing the findings of the *Times*' investigation into conditions at the site, in which they promote their march in support of the hunger strikers.

Polanski leads some 10,000 people through the streets of the small Kentish seaside town, waving a huge Refugee flag. Miles from central London, it is hard to get people to come out this far on a weekend for anything, let alone a political demonstration. Such is the level of anger and fear in the country.

'In a similar way as the Unite the Kingdom march had shown in the summer of 2025, the Manston march speaks to a strong anti-fascist pro-migrant movement, which is growing quickly,' one commentator for the *New Statesman* writes on X. Beside Polanski are people waving Palestinian, Scottish and LGBTQ+ flags. A banner across the bus states: 'Migrants Welcome Here! No One Is Illegal!' while others hold placards saying 'Migration Is What Makes This Country Great' and 'Refugees Welcome: Fight the Far-Right'. Another reads: 'Lee Anderson: This Crisis Is Of Your Making'.

All of the Green MPs walk with locked arms at the front of the march in a show of unity for a united party. During the election campaign, donations flooded into the Party's coffers. In autumn 2025, the Green Party took £4 million in membership fees in just 10 weeks after Polanski became leader. A fundraising drive before the election brought in another £25 million. The Party received dozens of celebrity endorsements – everyone from Dua Lipa to David Olusoga. Inspired by the strategy of Lib Dem Ed Davey at the 2024 election, they had organised a series of stunts to grab media attention that Polanski, a former immersive theatre actor, was only too happy to perform in. Polanski promoting the march and being front and centre for the cameras was part of that strategy, as well as being well in line with this agenda. Speaking into a loudhailer as the mass of people reach the open space of the airfield, Polanski says, 'The racists and xenophobes in Parliament do not define this country. This fight affects everyone – they're going to take away our human rights, start a trade war with Europe and deport your neighbours. The chaos at this terrible place is the direct result of a decision taken by one man: Lee Anderson, who has recklessly put the lives of people at risk for cheap political gain.'

As Polanski's words begin to make headlines on the homepages of the new sites on Fleet Street, a more genteel protest is happening in Trafalgar Square. Human Rights For All is organised by Amnesty International and Liberty. Many of the attendees are holding EU flags and Steve Bray, the Stop Brexit protester, is having his picture taken with people who have come into the capital today from the wealthier suburbs.

At first nobody noticed the actress Emma Thompson in the crowds arriving in oversized shades and a fake fur coat. She sidles up to a GB News interviewer and has a chat on camera: 'You're too young to remember Thatcher. Darling, it's just too awful! We're going back to those cruel days. Do you know what I call our new prime minister? I call him That Odious Man, TOM for short. What do you make of that? Quite good, isn't it?' She gives him a mischievous look.

Thompson is holding a placard saying: 'Say goodnight to Mr Tom' on it. She's wearing a pink hat with 'TOM' embroidered across it. GB News broadcasts the interview live interspersed with the increasingly chaotic scenes at Manston, as guards respond to a disturbance inside the detention centre. According to their reporter on the scene, a member of staff tried to force-feed one of the detainees, a fight had broken out and a mother had been tasered. One of the tents had somehow caught on fire and emergency evacuations were beginning.

Dan Jukes spots the clip of Thompson on the screen mounted in the Downing Street press room and issues a statement on behalf of the prime minister: 'Britain has had enough of being governed by left-wing luvvies like Ms Thompson. What is happening at Manston is a total disgrace and shows how the loony left are happy to leave the door open for those who wish to destroy our way of life. The protest will do nothing to stop our plans to deport every illegal migrant from Britain.'

At Manston, people sick of being held captive for weeks on end in squalid conditions run across the airfield to escape the fire. Guards shout at them to form orderly lines so they can be accounted for, but instead the asylum seekers mix with the crowd of demonstrators or run into the surrounding fields.

Faris jumps over a fence and heads for the road, desperately hoping to flag down another kind passer-by. Some protesters, sensing danger, are already running to the road to escape the inevitable arrival of the police. By the time the riot vans arrive, many of the demonstrators with peaceful intentions have left, leaving a core group in masks and goggles standing on the airstrip with a handful of asylum seekers who are livid at the authorities about their treatment. Cameramen and reporters try to get as close as possible to the action to broadcast live the horrific police charge which unfolds, attempting to broadcast the scenes of chaos for their viewers. The banner on GB News runs: 'The Battle of Manston: Illegals Assault Police In Migrant Centre Riot'. That evening, the channel carries images of the charred remains of the facility, placards scattered across the runway, and aerial footage of immigration vans scouring the Kent countryside for escapees, their headlights flashing in the dead of night.

8 p.m.

That evening, the government hurriedly announces it is bringing in legislation to amend the Terrorism Act 2000 to proscribe 'Our Rights' as a terrorist organisation and is designating detention centres as 'critical national infrastructure' in the same category as military airports, power stations and gas pipelines. When Starmer did the same to Palestine Action in 2025, the Labour government set a precedent that Reform are more than happy to follow. Anyone voicing support for Our Rights in 2029 risks prosecution and a jail sentence. One of the many measures the government can use against a proscribed group with impunity is the removal of any online content. After the vote was passed in the Commons, one of the largest human rights protest groups in the country was silenced overnight.

The Commissioner of the Metropolitan Police comments in an interview on LBC that cutting down the number of protests will go a long way towards saving precious policing resources. There are skirmishes in Trafalgar Square and Human Rights For All is also proscribed. The *New York Times* sends reporters to both events and publishes an article on the death of the right to protest in Britain, comparing the country to Orban's Hungary and Putin's Russia. That night there is fierce criticism of the Home Office for the premature closure of hotels, the collapse of order at Manston and the inhumane treatment of asylum seekers. The following morning, Lee Anderson announces his resignation.

Monday, 21 January 2030, 10 a.m.

The 'Battle of Manston' was on everyone's minds in Downing Street the next day. James Orr, a Farage advisor, was elevated to the Lords at a moment's notice and had been appointed the new home secretary. He is now sitting in the PM's office with Cummings in a meeting to decide once and for all how to quell resistance to the Great Repeal Bill in the Lords.

'Now's our chance,' Cummings says. 'We'll use the riot to our advantage – don't let a good crisis go to waste, Nigel. We should have done this in Covid but we used existing health legislation instead. Have you ever heard of the Civil Contingencies Act 2004?'

Using a whiteboard, Cummings begins to explain how the riot has given the Prime Minister the perfect opportunity. Farage could declare an official state of emergency under the Civil Contingencies Act (CCA) and he would have sweeping powers to enact policy with minimal parliamentary oversight.

'Thousands of illegals rioting on the streets of Kent surely meets the bar for the condition of serious public disorder under the Act,' Cummings says, scribbling acronyms and arrows on the board. He writes out the Act's definition of an emergency: 'An event or situation which threatens serious damage to human welfare in a place in the United Kingdom.'

If the CCA is activated, all a prime minister needs Parliament for is to renew the powers every month and even that can be delayed. The Lords are irrelevant. 'It's an incredibly powerful piece of legislation,' a parliamentary expert stated. The CCA's predecessor had been used five times by former PM Ted Heath in the 1970s, and also during the General Strike of 1926, when the sweeping freedom of speech restriction led to it being illegal to publicly criticise the government of the day. One communist was arrested while speaking at Hyde Park Corner.[19] The Act is intended to be used only for measures which mitigate the emergency, but in the eyes of Farage and Cummings, the only way to stop the boats is to pass the GRB and send in the Navy.

If the condition for an emergency is met, the government can legislate without the Commons, using an 'Order in Council'. This amounts to the Prime Minister and three or four other senior ministers who are members of the Privy Council meeting the King and requesting he sign the drawn-up orders, which can be about anything that is covered by normal primary legislation.

Just then, an official walks in and sees the Cy Twombly imitation on the whiteboard. She is able to deduce what they have been discussing and immediately starts laughing.

'Don't you know the one important thing about the CCA?' she says.

The prime minister and Cummings are silent.

'The only piece of legislation you can't use the CCA to get rid of is the Human Rights Act 1998. It's a Blair era law, it's useless for the purposes of getting the GRB though.'

---

[19]Shapurji Saklatvala, the first MP of Indian heritage, was arrested for sedition after speaking in support of miners.

The official exits the room, leaving the PM and Cummings with their heads in their hands, cursing the three-times Labour prime minister.

Farage's new home secretary now has a chance to pitch his proposal. James Orr outlines how the prime minister has the power to advise the King to create a whole host of life peers and there is nothing the monarch can do to refuse. Among those touted as potential Reform peers are the Brexiteer Andy Wigmore, QAnon hoax hotel owner John Mappin, key donor Jeremy Hosking and former Conservative minister Ann Widdecombe. There is no limit on the number Farage can create.

Orr outlines the political implications: the sight of some of the men and women they selected for peerages would inevitably face pushback. After he has submitted his choice to the King, it has to be vetted by the House of Lords appointments commission for proprietary and ethics. But Orr says, Farage doesn't actually have to pay any attention to that: under Boris Johnson, the committee was overruled on the appointment of Peter Cruddas, who had given £50,000 to Johnson for his leadership election campaign in 2019. The process can be fast: when David Cameron was raised to the Lords by Rishi Sunak and asked to serve as foreign secretary, the whole process was completed in a matter of weeks.

In the end, under immense political pressure exerted by the media, and widespread public frustration at the sight of the unelected chamber refusing to pass legislation which had been voted for by the public in an election and, in the eyes of many, would help solve the evident crisis at the border, the peers fold. The GRB passes the upper house after minimal amendments and becomes law. It will now be known as the Great Repeal Act.

The owner of the QAnon hotel John Mappin would have to wait another year to order his ermine.

WHAT IF REFORM WINS

Thursday, 26 September 2030, 12.45 p.m.

Despite the passage of the Bill, at first there is not much difference on the ground. Ministers have new legal powers, but Britain is still not a country of mass deportation. The Home Office is only now confident to start building 'UK Deportation Command', the ICE (US Immigration and Customs Enforcement)-style regime, to the designs of Farage and Cummings' imagination. Spin doctor Dan Jukes suggests to his boss that they reheat one of their favourite tactics: a trip from Dover on the English Channel to intercept small boats as they cross. They would invite GB News down to capture it all live. But this time, Jukes suggests they go one big step further.

What the Bill did allow was for the Navy to start repelling small boats in the Channel. In 2025, among former Border Force officials, sending in the Navy to stop the boats was met with wariness: former head of Border Force Tony Smith warned that it was 'bound by the law of the sea to rescue any person in danger in our territorial waters'.

'UKBF [UK Border Force] did try physical push-back trials under the last government, but the risk of drowning was found to be too high – and in that case we could be held culpable of causing death by drowning.' Farage is happy to ignore the United Nations maritime obligations – the obligation to help those at risk at sea is barely enforced. The other legal constraints preventing the Navy from repelling small boats – Article 3 Freedom for Torture and inhumane or degrading treatment and the Refugee Convention – no longer apply following the passing of the GRB.

The prime minister, wearing an admiral's cap, spots a migrant boat in the distance and commands the ship's Navy frigate captain to follow. The cameras would love it. The captain insists they keep a safe distance in case the wash from his far-larger vessel capsizes the fragile dinghy. After all the strife of the past year, Farage is like Nelson chasing Villeneuve and the Spanish Fleet on the High Seas. He has achieved what no one thought possible: as he looks out from his binoculars, he is master of all he surveys.

Friday, 27 September 2030, 8 a.m.

The British Ambassador in Paris is summoned next door on Rue du Faubourg Saint-Honoré to the Élysée Palace: the French are incandescent after Farage's vessel inadvertently strayed into their waters during the chase of the migrant dinghy the previous day.

Outside the Berlaymont building in Brussels, the EU's chief negotiator is on his way for breakfast at his favourite boulangerie when he is accosted by the *FT*'s man in the Belgian capital.

'Mr Sågfors![20] Have you seen the row between the British prime minister and the French? Any comment?'

'Yes, of course I have seen it,' he says, not noticing the reporter's iPhone camera. 'We keep a close eye on Mr Farage, here in Brussels.'

'Now that Britain is out of the ECHR, the country is technically in contravention of its trade agreement with Europe. Will you retaliate?'

'All options are on the table,' Sågfors says, and is about to say more when a colleague in the queue for coffee notices what is happening and gets rid of the reporter.

It takes less than an hour for the newspaper's homepage headline to read: 'EU Threatens Trade War As UK Becomes Human Rights Pariah'.

---

[20] Mr Sågfors is one of a few fictional inventions, for illustrative purposes.

Thursday, 24 October 2030

In the following months, the policy of mass deportation begins to take effect. In this scenario, the first person to be deported under the new rules is lauded by the press as a 'success for the Prime Minister' and 'proof his immigration legislation is watertight'. In the article, there were few details as to the person's identity beyond the facts that they were an 'illegal immigrant', had 'overstayed' their visa and had been caught while trying to 're-enter the UK at a London airport'.

The person not named is Bernadette Fernandes, a 70-year-old teacher and grandmother who first came to Britain from Goa in India during the pandemic. She lives near her daughter, son-in-law and her grandson in Ramsgate, Kent. Bernadette is a devout Catholic and St Ignatius church in the village had become her second home. She sits on the parish council, runs a much-loved curry stall at the school fête and was the lead organiser of the church's St Vincent de Paul Society, which visits isolated old people in the surrounding rural villages.

As she enters her seventies, she is spending more of her time looking after her teenage grandson because his father got a promotion at the local supermarket. Her grandson has profound and multiple learning disabilities and it is hard to trust anyone else to look after him. She is aware her visa is due to expire and as before, she applies to extend it but this time she is told new rules mean she does not meet the requirements. Nevertheless, she speaks to a lawyer friend of her daughter and re-applies.

The next month, her older sister dies in Germany. Catholic funerals happen fast and Bernadette's daughter helped her book a £40 flight to be there in time. Her visa situation doesn't enter her mind once as she dashes over to Hamburg. On her return, she is held at passport control at

Gatwick airport in a tiny room for hours. Bernadette goes into complete shock as the officers tell her she could be at risk of deportation. By going abroad, she has invalidated her application and is now an illegal immigrant. Under a Reform government, there is no mercy for such cases. She had of course seen that Farage had got into government and that they were making changes to the ECHR, but as an 'upstanding member of the community' she never thought the changes applied to her. Reform's constant talk of 'invaders' and sex offenders, as well as their paeans to the importance of Christianity to the nation's identity, had all given the impression that she would not be one of their targets. Her daughter turns up with Bernadette's lawyer, who explains there was an ongoing application for Bernadette to stay in the UK. The Border Force officers reluctantly allow her to go home on bail.

The following month, Bernadette's application is denied and she is told that if she stays in the UK, she will be in breach of the Great Repeal Act. The court ignores her claim that she has a right to stay in the UK to be near her family and that she has been in the country for nine years.

Cases like Bernadette's were already common in the immigration system. In 2023, immigration barristers in London represented an individual from a commonwealth country who had come to the country eight years previously, in 2016. Like Bernadette, they were well known in the community: they owned property, were members of their local church and were even a local councillor. They had permission to live in the UK on an entrepreneur visa, but the company eventually didn't make enough money to meet the requirements. They applied to stay but their application was not successful under the immigration rules and did not meet the criteria for Discretionary Leave, which is granted in exceptional circumstances. The individual was only permitted to stay in the UK as the Home

Office recognised that removing them would contravene their human rights under Article 8, the right to private and family life.

In 2030, with the Great Repeal Act enacted and Britain out of the ECHR, there are no such protections. There is nothing stopping the state from forcibly making Bernadette just another statistic in the figures supporting their ever expanding deportation regime.

4

Flood the Zone

SEVEN MONTHS EARLIER

Saturday, 23 February 2030, 11 a.m.

The Prime Minister is in a hard hat as he shakes the hand of an American fracking executive in a waterlogged field in his home county.

'I'm a Kentish lad,' he tells the assembled media in his speech. 'I was born in Farnborough, I fish with my son in the Darent, I walk my dogs here on the weekends. I'll be inviting you later for a pint of Spitfire at my former local. I care deeply about this county, but the Garden of England is special for another reason. It has a God-given chance to contribute something incredible to this country: to win energy independence and lower bills for Britain. We are standing today on the Jurassic Weald Belt. For nearly two decades, successive British governments have banned any exploration of the bounty that could lie below our very feet. Meanwhile, millions of pensioners go without heating in winter, while manufacturing – in a country which invented the steam engine and built the modern world – is crying out for cheaper bills. It is lunacy that we have the highest industrial energy prices in the world, all because of Labour's net zero obsession and their ideological addiction to impractical and costly renewable energy.

'We announced our intentions for a Great Climate Repeal Bill in the King's Speech and within that legislation, we intend to reverse the permanent ban on fracking and stipulate measures which encourage shale gas exploration here in the South, but also across Yorkshire, Lancashire and Cheshire. Under Reform, we want to make Britain the Abu Dhabi of shale gas. But we have a bit of catching up to do!

'To all the media here today: keep your hats on, we're not going to cause any earthquakes. Before you write your articles, talk to some of the men and women I've invited here today, who are doing good business in America and elsewhere, and are paying their governments billions in tax. And they're so happy to hand it over, aren't you guys?' Farage says as the executives chuckle.

'My friends from California will tell you about wells in downtown Beverly Hills, Los Angeles, which I have visited, which were once quite literally opposite the local shopping mall. Until 10 years ago, you could frack beside people's homes and the disturbances would be no more than the vibration of the trucks carrying sets to the studios in Hollywood. Here in Britain, anyone who has ever lived in a mining community will tell you that the odd little shake is part and parcel of daily life. Today we are lifting the ban on fracking, but we are going to go further: my party will pay communities that support planning applications for new wells with money off their energy bills worth £400 per family. We will also give a special offer to local landowners and energy companies to allow them to keep more of a share of the revenues from fracking. But only if they get cracking with their applications for exploration on their fields within the next year. Reform is committed to seeing this industry grow and we want local communities in Kent and everywhere else this opportunity exists to benefit. Who knows? Maybe we'll see property prices soar as people realise how much money they could be saving by moving here. I'm delighted to be standing on the first exploration site with the CEO of EQT Corporation, all the way from Pittsburgh, Pennsylvania, who will now tell you more about his plans here.'

It begins to drizzle as the shale gas executive thanks Farage and the team from Downing Street rush to find an umbrella.

11.05 a.m.

The Party's new secretary of state for energy, Baroness Andrea Jenkyns, applauds the prime minister from the front row. At the King's Speech, presented at the State Opening of Parliament two weeks after the election, the monarch announced the government's intention to introduce a 'Great Climate Repeal Bill'. Despite protestations that morning from the Lord Speaker, Jenkyns had posed for photographs in the chamber in traditional ermine robes emblazoned with 'drill baby drill'. Afterwards, she told the media in the Central Lobby in Westminster that Reform had 'declared war' on green energy projects, GB Energy, Natural England and the Environment Agency. Renewables provided a 'pathetic amount of power compared to what we need,' she said. 'When the wind doesn't blow, we pay astronomical sums, and then when it's too windy, we also have to cough up. And they demand we spend billions updating the grid. Frankly, it's a joke. We love gas because it always works, whether there's wind, sun, or none at all. And by the way, AI is going to pass us right by. It already has. You've seen the stories of AI companies buying gas power plants and small nuclear reactors to run their data centres for themselves. The way things are now, renewable energy is costing Britain its future – the eco-lobby in this country is a cult, and we're calling time on it.'

As she was speaking to the camera, Leader of the Liberal Democrats, Ed Davey, walked behind her in the lobby. He seemed to mutter something to himself, which the microphone did not pick up, but Jenkyns heard. She broke away from the interview and called after him. 'You should be a pariah for how much subsidy money you handed out when you were the energy minister in 2013. Shame! Shame on you, Ed Davey!' she shouted after him as he hurried away to a select committee on tree planting.

Following the King's Speech, Farage's assault on nature and the climate had provided a shot in the arm for Britain's climate protest movement. A Just Stop Oil offshoot, Planet Justice, had staged a mass 'die in' at the Reform Party Conference the previous autumn when Farage discussed the Great Climate Repeal Bill (GCRB) in his speech, which had to be postponed after one of the exhibition centre's security guards assaulted a protesting grandmother wearing a crocheted hat, and a priest covered in pin badges.

After the activists had been dragged from the hall, Farage had set out in more detail what the GCRB would contain. It would replace the Climate Change Act 2008, which drives progress towards Britain becoming 'net zero' by 2050, in the statute books. Scrapping the legislation would allow Farage to act quickly to reverse climate measures with less risk of judicial review. It also meant the abolition of carbon budgets, which set legally binding targets on emission reductions, and it would also overturn recent Labour legislation so that ministers would be able to issue new licences for North Sea oil exploration and reverse the effective bans on some fossil fuels, allowing for new coal-fired power plants and fracking. The Reform delegates at conference rose to their feet for a five-minute standing ovation as their leader promised a 'second British Industrial Revolution powered by energy from cheap coal and reliable gas'.

There were a number of things Farage could point to that he had immediately done to destroy net zero without the need for primary legislation. On entering office, the prime minister had swiftly announced the defunding of programmes insulating homes and installing heat pumps. Reform legislation also targeted Natural England and the Environment Agency, which are responsible for protecting Britain's environment and responding to floods and pollution events.

'The lunacy of Britain's biggest quangos forcing us to spend £100 million on bat tunnels and to write 55,000 pages for a planning application for a nuclear power plant is over. We're going to have a huge battle on our hands – the bureaucracy isn't going to give up its power easily. There will need to be purges, we're going to have to just clear people out,' Farage had stated on his daily TikTok show. His attacks on bat tunnels and other biodiversity regulation were close to what Labour had been saying under Keir Starmer and before the election. The prime minister decided to leave the Environment Agency's flood budget alone: in case of an emergency, he needed political cover. But he ordered brutal cuts to all other parts of the organisation, with employees at its HQ in Bristol immediately launching a strike in protest. There had been howls of outrage from the 11 Green MPs in Parliament, but in the honeymoon period after the election, and still riding high in the polls, Farage felt he could do no wrong.

By the spring of 2030, however, progress on the Great Climate Repeal Bill had slowed. He had already gone for the low-hanging fruit but he needed to go further. Reform were finding that scrapping laws and passing new ones was more complicated than it looked at first. At the first Budget in the autumn of 2029, Tice had begun to make changes. He had consulted with the oil companies in Scotland and handed them a cut in the windfall tax of 20 per cent. The 'Drill Baby Drill' cut, as the newspapers called it, was approved by the Conservatives, who wanted to appear pro-growth and had already jettisoned their green credentials under Kemi Badenoch. But Reform donors with connections to the fossil fuel industry were disappointed Tice had not gone further and reversed the full increase imposed by the Tories in 2022. The chancellor had lost his courage when Treasury officials pointed out to him that scrapping the tax rise entirely would cost £3 billion. To make it up to the donors, he revealed new taxes on Britain's biggest renewable energy companies. They didn't net the Exchequer very much, but they were meant to begin the process of unwinding what he saw as the gravy train of green subsidies.

Which must be why, Jenkyns reflects from the front row of Farage's speech in Kent, today feels like they're finally breaking ground. Fracking would be back for good.

12 p.m.

In the audience, lobbyists in new waxed jackets and Wellingtons swell the ranks of the audience and join the rest of Reform as they walk to The Rifleman pub in the downpour.

Two 'think-tanks' in particular are out in force. The Global Warming Policy Foundation (GWPF) and Net Zero Watch (NZW) had worked tirelessly to put forward climate-sceptic arguments in the press and to politicians. Their strategy was to talk less about climate as according to them it 'makes people's eyes glaze over'. Instead they focused on how much net zero policies could cost the public at a time when the cost of living was high.

Headquartered at 55 Tufton Street in Westminster, GWPF and NZW are part of a stable of organisations, including Big Brother Watch, No2ID, Migration Watch, Civitas, New Culture Forum and the TaxPayersAlliance, which work to advance the right in Britain. These 'dark money' groups share a policy of never declaring who their funders are, raising questions of who is benefiting from their extreme agenda. According to one Tufton Street staffer, up until 2023, his group were 'on the margins' due to a 'watertight consensus' on the need for Britain to be a global leader on climate action. He told how they had worked with Conservative MPs to chip away at the public's assumptions, launching campaigns against electric vehicle quotas and heat pumps, as well as supporting the nascent fracking industry. They saw success: the rebellion against Rishi Sunak over electric vehicles was the second largest of his premiership. Speak to them and they will say a key turning point was the former prime minister's decision to delay the planned ban on petrol cars and requirements for the replacement of gas boilers. Sunak, who belonged to the same party which had passed net zero by 2050 legislation in 2019, had in one stroke legitimised the view that stopping climate change was an economic burden.

On the demise of the Tories, the groups switched allegiance to Reform. In 2025, Tufton Street directors exchanged regular WhatsApps with Tice on energy and other issues.

'We talk to each other and we're all singing from the same hymn sheet,' said one informal Reform advisor belonging to an organisation hoping to influence the Party's policy.

2 p.m.

After the speech, in a nook of The Rifleman, Farage's new home secretary James Orr holds court to a group of party donors. They think Orr, who is one month into the job, is very clever. The secretary of state is a former professor of theology at Cambridge, a staunch Christian and a one-time mentor to the President of the United States JD Vance, with whom he partied in the Cotswolds on Vance's visit to the UK in the summer of 2025. The donors listen intently as he explains his theory of the connections between net zero, Christianity and 'transgenderism'.

'British culture is in peril and net zero is part of that. Look at the videos of phone snatching – Americans won't come here because they're too afraid. Look at demographic decline, look at our universities ... Energy is the master resource: if we reverse net zero and reverse economic decline, we can fund a renewal of British Christian civilisation. I see all these woke beliefs – environmentalism, transgenderism – as mere post-Christian offshoots. This is about so much more than digging stuff up out of the ground: if we get this right, your companies will be part of driving paganism out of this country for good.'

He continues to ramble on as another donor returns with a fourth round. Around the table sit some of Reform's largest donors, many of whom have connections with the fossil fuel industry. In 2025, openDemocracy's work investigating the background of Reform donors helped point to the reasons for the Party's keenness to see an end to renewables and action on climate change. The same year, David Lilley, a long-time hedge fund boss, gave £274,000 to the Party. His firms, Red Kite and Drakewood Capital Management, have interests in mining and metals trading. First Corporate Consultants, which gave £200,000, is owned by Terence Mordaunt, a former chair of the Global Warming Policy Foundation (GWPF). In 2022, openDemocracy showed that GWPF, whose trustees included Nigel Lawson and Steve Baker, was funded by an oil-rich foundation with investments in polluting companies and indirectly through the billionaire, climate-sceptic Koch brothers. Jeremy Hosking, an asset manager and political donor, has given the party £140,000. His fund reportedly has tens of millions invested in oil companies and the broader fossil fuel industry. Hosking donated to the Vote Leave campaign and is a major funder of Laurence Fox's Reclaim Party. Other funders include Nova Venture Holdings, part of a portfolio of companies run by energy executive Jacques Tohme, who campaigns on behalf of the North Sea oil and gas industry.

James Orr finishes his speech and invites his audience to a £2,000-a-ticket networking event he is hosting. For face-time with ministers happy to cut corners on contracts and turn a blind eye to the regulations, the CEOs considered it a bargain.

5 p.m.

The Rifleman's landlord sets up a gazebo outside to accommodate the many smokers in the torrential rain. Underneath stands Baroness Jenkyns, enjoying a celebratory cigarette: she was delighted that her advisors managed to work with No 10 to get the prime minister to announce their key growth policy. Jenkyns was one of Farage's favourites: he wanted her in the Cabinet, but she'd had only just stepped down as Mayor of Greater Lincolnshire a month before the election and didn't have a seat, so he raised her to the Lords and made her energy minister. In 2025, the Baroness had impressed his inner circle when, at a press conference to launch a campaign against a solar farm in Lincolnshire, she likened the fight against green energy to the actions of RAF Bomber Command, which was based in the county during the Second World War. She said she wanted to 'unleash the spirit of Lincolnshire' against the 'planned desecration of our countryside'. It was exactly that sort of talk which Reform needed if they were going to take on what they called the 'eco-lobby'.

In 2024, when Ed Miliband arrived at the Department for Energy and Net Zero on the day after the election, such was the euphoria and relief from officials that some were seen crying as they applauded his debut speech. Things were very different when Jenkyns arrived at the office opposite Horse Guards on Whitehall. She sat in the empty space with her two special advisors, both of whom were former NZW staffers. Her first decision was to cut 'and Net Zero' from the department's name and the second was to have officials look into how many renewable energy contracts she could shut down immediately. Her private office had come back the next morning with nervous expressions. They told her she could effectively scrap contracts for subsidy arrangements from before 2017, which make up 20 per cent of the total. They said she could cancel any further renewable energy auctions. But more recent contracts for wind and solar were locked in until at least 2037 and beyond. They had a contractual right to the subsidy, first agreed under the Coalition government. Successive ministers had agreed long-term deals to guarantee a price for renewable energy, as opposed to oil and gas, which is set on the global market. Contracts with wind farms which require changes to the National Grid can run on even longer. The Energy Trading Scheme, an offset market which caps emissions for polluting sectors like aviation and power generation, was set down in statute and would need primary legislation to scrap.

At one meeting soon after the election, Jenkyns banged her fist on the table as she realised how difficult it would be to roll back parts of the energy transition. One Reform-supporting think-tank employee fretted that the Party would be in 'deep shit' come the next election, given how 'extremely difficult' it was to unpick Britain's energy commitments. 'You essentially can't change anything,' he said.

'But Parliament's sovereign,' one of the SoS advisors in the department protested to his minister. He cited a decades-old court case where it was decided the government had to pay compensation to the owner of a well destroyed in the

Second World War and Parliament responded with the War Damages Act, which said it did not have to pay compensation in times of war.

Surely Parliament could just annul the contracts?

'We could say, "This is a catastrophe. We're heading towards economic ruin if we don't do this,"' the advisor suggested.

The officials fell silent for a moment, thinking how best to tell the advisor what an insane argument this was. The contracts had been made with a private company, the Low Carbon Contracts Company, owned by the Department for Energy and Net Zero: legislating to exempt the country from legal action was not only unconstitutional but would destroy private sector confidence in British contract law. Getting business done with anyone would become almost impossible. The agreements were created in this way explicitly to ensure that renewable energy projects had full contract law rights so future governments couldn't disrupt them, an idea which has since been copied internationally. What company would work with a government which reneged on its contractual commercial obligations? Investors would have ministers up in front of a tribunal within weeks and could point to the Energy Charter Treaty to make their case.

Officials take Jenkyns' special advisors aside and warn that messing around with the contracts could spook the market. But there are signs that Reform and Tice are already thinking about this: in July 2025, the MP wrote a letter to eight leading energy firms warning that to bid for new contracts carried 'significant' risk that they would be ripped up under a Reform government. One Party observer said this was so that, in office, Tice could point to the letter in court and say to the companies: 'You were warned.'

The next day, Jenkyns ordered her permanent secretary to fire or reshuffle all the private secretaries in her office, whom she accused of giving 'obstructive advice' on a key manifesto pledge to abolish renewable energy contracts.

8 p.m.

At the pub, Jenkyns listens as a shale gas executive from Texas extols the prime minister's announcement while propping up the bar with his sixth pint of lager. 'Even before, when this tech was here, you guys never really had it. There were so many rules on it, way more than for geothermal. If you're in geothermal, you could trigger tremors and they wouldn't care. But when people hear you're fracking, they lose their minds in this country! When you're in fracking, you're always trying to find the right recipe for your shale to deliver up its gas, and if you can't even explore to find out what's down there, what's the point? Money's gonna flow, Andrea, you'll see. I've just been speaking to that guy from Cuadrilla ...'

They look over to the corner of the room, where the chief executive of Britain's only fracking company is swaying at the other end of the bar, talking to Lord Offord, Reform's leader in Scotland and a former shadow energy minister. In 2011, Cuadrilla caused a minor earthquake measuring 2.3 on the Richter scale after fracking in Lancashire. There was an intense public backlash and the Conservative government responded by imposing a moratorium on any further exploration.

'He's been sitting on remarkable tests for years, decades. Not allowed to do a thing about them until today,' the Texan says.

Monday, 25 February 2030, 8.30 a.m.

The next morning, Baroness Jenkyns is still nursing a faint hangover as the ministerial car pulls up outside her house in the torrential rain that continues to fall on London. Inside, her special advisor is already waiting to present her with research carried out on the potentially huge unemployment spike which could result from Jenkyns' fight with the renewable energy market. Over 100,000 people could lose their jobs across the country. Renewable manufacturers Siemens Gamesa in Hull and Vestas on the Isle of Wight will immediately write to Downing Street to warn about layoffs, she warns. In Lincolnshire, Jenkyns' former mayoralty region, net zero contributed nearly £1 billion to the local economy and employed over 12,000 people. Is the minister sure her party will go along with her views? In 2025, Reform had splits on fracking with Reform-controlled Lancashire County Council voting against plans to give Cuadrilla more time to restore a former fracking site back to farmland. Despite the Party's national policy, the council's Reform Cabinet member for the environment said fracking 'has been proven in Lancashire not to be safe.'

Jenkyns' advisor suggests a 'phased approach' which concentrates on building more 'firm' power, like fossil fuels and nuclear, while they attempt to wind down renewables. But now she is in the House of Lords, Baroness Jenkyns has to worry less about what the people of Lincolnshire think, and besides, the British public voted for these measures at the election. With the rise of fracking, exploration in the North Sea and industry flourishing again with cheap energy, there would be plenty of new jobs to go around, she tells her advisor.

'I also have to tell you a bit of bad news. After we left the field in Kent yesterday, local activists went around and leafletted every village in a five-mile radius, saying that Nigel Farage was going to poison their water and they should be careful drinking it,' the advisor continues.

She shows the Baroness a video posted to social media of queues of people outside nearby supermarkets stocking up on bottled water: 'There's also now an encampment on the landowner's field by local hippies, who claim it has spiritual significance.'

After the event, local WhatsApp groups had lit up with vows to submit planning objections to block any potential well in the area, and campaigners for the protest group Frack Off set up a stall in the local market to tell shoppers about the risk to the Garden of England. Articles in which people could submit their postcode to discover 'how much Angela Jenkyns' fracking policy is going to take off your house price' were already starting to go up online.

'At least the Texans have left …'

'Well, actually, activists slashed the tyres on their Chryslers and the hotel asked them to leave because of the chaos. One of the government drivers picked them up on the side of the road but they still missed their flight to Dallas.'

The advisor can't help letting out a small laugh.

'It's not funny. This is what we're up against – utter hysteria and mendacity. Don't you have anything good to tell me?' Jenkyns snaps. Everything felt beset by difficult and insurmountable process. The minister was sick of hearing 'no'.

The advisor pulls out a file printed on Foreign Office paper. Inside are documents relating to the Sea Lion oil field, 136 miles north of the Falkland Islands. Discovered in 2010 by Rockhopper, 65 per cent of it is owned by Navitas Petroleum, an Israeli company. The proposals had been green-lit under Keir Starmer's government, but in 2028 at the last minute the Labour foreign secretary changed his mind and the project had ground to a halt. One of the pages was a letter from the Israelis, making a 'last-ditch' plea to the British government to green-light the project, pointing out that the vast majority of Falkland Islanders were keen for them to get drilling. Since 2025, the company had done further investigations and found the field was much larger than previously thought – the rewards for the Exchequer and the country's finance would be immeasurable. In 2025, the company predicted there were 300 million barrels of extractable oil available out of a total of 900 million, but in 2029, with new technology, they believed they could extract double their original estimate. Jenkyns didn't know why her predecessor had suddenly stalled the project, but there were obvious sensitivities with the Argentine government.

While President Milei might be on the same page economically as them, Jenkyns knew that the Argentines were the sworn enemy of the British. Jenkyns had been eight in 1982 when she watched Thatcher receiving the salute in the City of London from the returning seamen and marines after their victory. The previous summer, in the run-up to the election, she had joined Farage and other like-minded Reform members at a tea party at Raffles to celebrate 50 years since Thatcher's election in May 1979.

In 2025, the Foreign Office was reluctant to back the project because of this sensitive situation with the Argentine government. One Reform watcher at the time said a Farage-led government 'would be up for' seeing the project go ahead so they could capitalise on the tax revenue.

In the back of the government car, Jenkyns considers the chaos that was in store across the country if these fracking protests groups continued their campaign. It was out of the question to pull the policy, but it would be politically useful for her to be able to point to how Reform was winning big for the British people. And in the south Atlantic, she muses longingly, there would be no difficult NIMBYs to fight.

Meanwhile, observers of Argentine politics noted that the country's maverick president Javier Milei clearly felt emboldened to make ever more audacious comments on the sovereignty of 'Islas Malvinas'. Back in September 2025, he had claimed that the islands were 'illegally occupied' at the UN. There was no suggestion that he would try to take the islands, journalists agreed, but with an election only 18 months away in 2031 and his party lagging in the polls, a clash with the British might work in their favour.

Jenkyns prepares herself for the morning's Cabinet meeting. In Starmer's Downing Street, Cabinet was often structured through a series of 'turn-tos', where the prime minister would in advance invite a few ministers to speak to an agenda item, which was usually an opportunity for the minister to supply their boss with a supportive comment. Under Farage, order in Cabinet had broken down as the mostly male ministers randomly interjected over one another for attention.

This time, Jenkyns manages to get a word in by extolling the prime minister's ability to bring business people together.

'This is why it's so important that we have a former businessman like the prime minister in this building. And as a businessman, I thought he would be interested in documents I've been presented about a horrific business call made by the previous government.' She brings out the Foreign Office file and describes the 'goldmine lying in our waters', warning that if the government doesn't act to encourage drilling and strike a deal on tax with the Islanders, they could miss out entirely.

Farage loves the plan, and despite an attempted interjection from Danny Kruger, the foreign secretary, who has been positioned down the far end of the table, he tells Jenkyns to prioritise getting a deal.

Tuesday, 26 February 2030, 2 p.m.

The Ambassador to Argentina demands to see the foreign secretary.

'How dare you insult the delicate peace our two countries have enjoyed for nearly half a century! We leave each other alone and now your mad energy secretary wants to take all the oil for herself. I told your predecessor, do not risk it. Do not poke the bear. My president, he's just as mad as she is. If you go ahead with this deal in Islas Malvinas then we will surely have to start preparing our troops ...'

'We will never be bullied by Argentines. Your lot learnt the hard way the last time. We'll stick it up you once again if you're not bloody careful! Listen to me, go back to your president and tell him, he can do whatever he wants. A new administration is in charge now and we do things differently. And if we want to drill, we will.'

The foreign secretary retold the story to hoots of laughter at a meeting with Farage later that day. It was one of his finest performances.

Meanwhile, the secretary for war secretly phones the heads of the Army and Navy, and tells them to ready their men and women – just in case.

Wednesday, 27 February 2030, 12 p.m.

At PMQs, half the benches in the Commons are empty when the Speaker calls the prime minister. In London, six lines on the Underground are down due to flash flooding and the roads around Westminster have become rivers as drains block and overflow. Carla Denyer, the re-elected MP for Bristol Central, stands to lambast Farage for slashing the Environment Agency's overall budget during the climate crisis:

'The Prime Minister is blind to what is happening to this very city. Look around: the effects of climate change are creating havoc for Londoners today. Next week, Storm Octavia is predicted to batter the west of England.'

Reform MPs, when they hear Denyer has wasted her one question at PMQs on the subject of inclement weather, start talking among themselves about their difficult journeys and moaning constituents.

'My constituents are terrified of the predictions for record rain and potential flooding along the River Avon and Bristol Channel. If the Seabank power station is hit, this could take out electricity for nearly a third of the city. This is not to mention the threat to the Hinkley Point nuclear power stations which sit right on the Channel. But as the secretary of state for energy is in the Lords, she is not here to heed this warning,' Denyer says. There are sounds of mock surprise from her Green colleagues. 'Will the prime minister convene a COBRA meeting to address the rain …'

The Speaker cuts her off to protest against a Reform MP taking a selfie on their iPad. MPs on all sides of the House laugh as Denyer struggles to finish her question. She gives up and sits and waits for the prime minister's answer.

'This is Britain. It rains sometimes, alright love? But, yes, any impacts from floods will be dealt with. We've protected those budgets from cuts. Probably'll fare even better this year, following the efficiencies we've made to the Environment Agency'.

Monday, 4 March 2030, 9 p.m.

In this scenario, Kent County Council (KCC)'s former cabinet member for the environment has been appointed as the minister for water and food security. Secretary of State David Wimble is sitting in a traffic jam caused by surface flooding near Paddington. On the radio, the presenter says there are 40 active severe flood warnings around the country, nearly all in the west of England. Wimble is driving back from a National Farmers Union (NFU) event to his flat in Ealing: he eschews the ministerial car in favour of his preferred mode of transport, a London taxi cab with a turquoise Union Jack skin which he bought during his election campaign. On the side is printed: 'Let's save Britain'. He finds it goes down very well with the right people, which for him is what being a politician is all about.

Wimble had been chosen as a candidate along with many other former KCC councillors and had been praised by the Party's top brass for rescinding the council's 'climate emergency' declaration almost immediately on taking office in September 2025. 'Nature will do what nature does,' his boss Linden Kemkaran said of climate change at the time. Wimble turns off the ignition, sits in the jam, and begins to compose a post on X, something he does dozens of times a day. As a former newspaper editor, he is more than happy to share his views with all the new followers he's acquired since becoming a minister. It reads: 'It's very wet today – my thoughts are with everyone driving home in this. Yes, there is climate change, there always has been. The planet has gone through cycles of warming and cooling for millions of years. In fact, around 400 years ago Britain's average temperature was two degrees hotter than it is today! That's not politics, that's history. It's called the course of nature. Seeing lots of people on my timeline saying it's raining because of a "climate emergency". Maybe, just maybe, instead of running around screaming, we should focus on balance – real science, not fearmongering. Because the word "emergency" spreads panic, not progress. Calm down, everyone. Share if you agree.'

He sends the post, thinking about the civil servants – many of whom he is certain are covert Greenpeace activists – who have been sending him countless emails that day about the bad weather in the West. Protocol in the Department for Water and Food Security dictates that the secretary of state and the floods minister be kept up to date with the latest predictions from the Met Office and receive a document telling them what the potential for flooding is, where it is expected to hit, at what time, which areas will be the worst affected and what preparations have been done ahead of it. A team of officials in the department is stood up, and if the flood is severe enough, it will be declared a critical or major incident.

Wimble had declined calls from his officials to be in the department that day as he had had an appointment to ride a tractor with the head of the NFU. The *Telegraph* story was already up online. As he went to refresh notifications to check reactions to his post, a call flashes up on the minister's phone from a former Conservative donor based in the Cotswolds who switched to Reform and helped him win his seat.

'If I was you, Dave, I'd get down to Bristol. It's looking pretty dicey down there and the station might not be open for long. It will look really bad if the minister isn't wearing wellies and carrying sandbanks in a few days.'

Wimble, who has only been an MP for under a year, let alone a minister, takes the donor's advice seriously. When the traffic starts moving again, he turns and heads for the station, boarding the first train he can to Bristol.

10 p.m.

It's not until he's past Reading that he tells his advisors what he's done – 'Private office are not going to like it.' As predicted, Wimble receives a call a few minutes later to say it was 'against protocol' for a minister to visit a flood zone based on weather warnings alone: 'It confuses things. Best to leave it two or three days. You might hinder the response because they'll have to babysit you instead of helping people,' the principal private secretary (PPS) explains. But by now the PPS is used to his minister throwing all caution to the wind.

For politicians, the decision on how to approach a crisis zone is fraught with political risk: in 2017, Jeremy Corbyn won praise for embracing residents of Grenfell Tower after the blaze, whereas Theresa May acted on security advice and was criticised for not meeting survivors.

'You're too late, I'm nearly at Didcot,' Wimble tells his principal private secretary.

Wimble peers out of the window and sees the light from the train reflected on the fields: in the dark, it seems as if Oxfordshire and Gloucestershire have become great lakes, the lights of distant villages like buoys in the water. There's a new moon and the stars are covered by thick cloud. When he gets off at Temple Meads, he calls his advisor again, but the wind is so fierce he is forced to abandon it.

'This is more serious than we thought,' he texts. 'Please get here as soon as possible tomorrow.'

11.30 p.m.

Wimble is met at the station by two drenched Environment Agency (EA) officers, who whisk the minister to the operations room at the national headquarters of the organisation, just off College Green. The water is rising quickly in the area towards the harbour to the south, but the EA HQ and the cathedral are safe, for now. Despite the crisis, Wimble notices that the office is emptier than expected. At first, he assumes it must be due to the storm, but an official informs him that it is as much to do with budget cuts.

A Reform administration would have 'a lot' of power over the EA, a senior government source said. 'You have ministerial directions. You can basically write and direct them to do something.' But in the event of an emergency, the real pain could come as a result of wider personnel cuts across the Agency. 'A lot of people who aren't [in floods teams] help during an emergency and have in their contract they will help out of hours. If you're an air quality person in the EA, you've probably done some training to help during a flood emergency, so it's not just floods people that help during flooding, it's anybody who works in the Environment Agency. If you cut away the Environment Agency down to just a flooding department, and get rid of everyone else, which [Farage] could potentially do, then your capacity to respond during a flood emergency is much more limited.'

The people who would have been there before to help put a flood barrier up along the Avon have, in 2030, been sacked or made redundant, while the others are out on strike against Farage and Tice's cuts.

11.40 p.m.

Wimble is silent as he is told that the area around Bristol is forecast to experience over six weeks' worth of rain in the next 24 hours, which is due to fall on already water-logged land. The Met Office says the downpour will be even greater than the Great Storm of 1968 when the River Chew broke its banks. On the TV screen, a muted BBC weather presenter waves his hand over a sea of red weather warnings covering the whole of the west and south of England.

Ministers visiting floods are always immediately met by the most senior person on the scene, but this usually happens after the worst is over and the area is out of crisis. The operations lead from the Environment Agency in Bristol brings Wimble into a small empty office, locks the door, and produces a series of documents and forecast models on an iPad. 'We are in the middle of a deadly mix of high winds and high tides, which is likely to lead to a storm surge, hitting Avonmouth on the Channel first,' he says, pointing to their location. Wimble nods along, trying to look convincing as the man in front of him babbles about storm surges and mitigation strategies.

Storm surges occur when a low-pressure weather system and strong winds force an extremely high spring tide to rise far beyond predictions, overwhelming defences and bringing devastation in its wake. They are increasing around the world in frequency and intensity due to the warming planet. Bristol is particularly susceptible. The Bristol Channel's unique funnel shape concentrates water into an ever narrower space as the tide comes in, meaning that water rises up from the seabed higher than elsewhere. The Channel has the second largest tidal range, or the distance between high and low tide, in the world. The funnelling effect also increases the speed of the incoming water, especially if there is a high spring tide when more water is being forced into the area. With water levels elevated by the Channel's shape and the stage of the Moon, it makes the prospect of catastrophic flooding occurring during a bad storm possible. In 1607, the Channel was the scene of Britain's worst natural disaster when 2,000 people were killed when a spring high tide of 7.86m combined with a violent storm. In such a moment, the tide would push huge amounts of water up the River Avon and into the city centre.

Wimble listens to all this with his head in his hands and takes a gulp from an Environment Agency mug which has 'solar-powered building, tea-powered staff' written on it.

11.43 p.m.

'We are also concerned about the possibility of tidal locking,' the operations lead tells the minister, who is looking dazed from the deluge of information he is expected to take in. Wimble wishes he had just gone home. The thought of going on the broadcast round the next day to explain all this makes him feel sick. His was meant to be one of the easy jobs – the quangos would look after the hard stuff and the prospect of Reform actually nationalising the water companies as they'd claimed they wanted to do in the election was slim. Now he was being told by dozens of people in high-vis that Britain's eighth-largest city was facing a once-in-200-years catastrophe.

'Tide locking occurs when a high sea level, like tonight, stops rivers from draining out to sea, meaning they back up and cause the river to flood the whole surrounding area.'

Behind him, on a screen, there is an interactive map of Bristol where whole swatches are covered in purple. It is a flood map predicting a scenario not meant to happen for another 70 years: on screen, the Arnolfini art gallery, the Old Vic theatre, even the grounds near the Cathedral, are all underwater. 'It could get that bad tonight,' the man from the Environment Agency says. He points to the parts of the city nearest the harbour: 'The most economically valuable parts of the city centre are completely undefended; Temple Meads will become inaccessible; a third of the roads will be deluged, including the underpass connecting the main road to London with the city. The city is a sitting duck.'

The minister, cogent of the fact Reform had made swingeing cuts to the Environment Agency in Tice's first Budget, texts Downing Street's director of communications, Dan Jukes, to prepare for the media fallout the next day.

Tuesday, 5 March 2030, 1 a.m.

Wimble is shown a video, shot by an intrepid farmer with a strong torch, of a tributary of the River Avon which has now become a violent torrent of water and debris. A dozen of the man's cows lie dead on the banks and it's clear he is struggling against the wind to stay upright.

'The storm is tracking eastwards, with gales expected to peak at some point in the early hours of this morning,' the operations lead says. 'In the first instance, we are prioritising the protection of life and critical infrastructure. We are particularly concerned about Seabank Power Station and an electricity substation in Avonmouth which powers between 20 and 30 per cent of the city. We are taking the immediate decision to close Temple Meads tonight – it is situated at one of the lowest points in the city centre and will become dangerous tomorrow if the water continues to rise.'

'Would you be able to wait for the first train to arrive so my advisor can come?'

'I'm afraid that's out of the question.'

'What if it had the prime minister on it?' Wimble asks.

The operations lead looks at his deputy, who seems uncertain, but agrees to divert extra resources to keep the station open for Farage, if he decides to come.

One of the operations managers suggests they take the minister to show him the damage and begins looking for a high-vis jacket in his size, but his boss stops him: 'Minister, why don't you go to your hotel with one of the drivers and we'll see you in the morning?'

4 a.m.

Meanwhile, in Downing Street, one of the private secretaries knocks on the bedroom door of the prime minister's apartment in No 11. Farage had returned late to the residence after enjoying a long weekend in France with his wife Laure's family and turned his phone off so he could catch up on sleep.

'Prime Minister, it's Baroness Jenkyns on the phone for you. It's about floods in Bristol. She's had a call from the

National Grid saying they're worried about a third of Bristol losing power. They're getting pretty battered over there.'

'Bristol?' Farage has tried to put the city out of his mind since the election, where he made an ill-thought-through campaign visit to support a candidate. He'd had another milkshake thrown at him and was mobbed by pro-Gaza activists. Reform had no voters in Bristol, so why was he being woken up about it at 4 a.m.?

He pulls on a dressing gown and heads downstairs. Flooding happens every single year. Farage reminds his private secretary that he's the prime minister: could this not be left to the Department to handle?

But by the time he's made it to his office, the official present has told him that in order to meet with the relevant people he needs, Farage had best convene COBR. The meetings tend to occur in a set of rooms in the Cabinet Office in 70 Whitehall, where no phones are allowed and which are routinely swept for bugs. Each room has a different level of security and is used for varying levels of crisis. A photo of one COBR room released under a Freedom of Information Request in 2010 shows 22 black high chairs around a large table with eight screens at one end. Those who have attended the meetings recently say it is someone's job to live type what is being discussed so it appears as ministers and officials discuss a response. As each department goes through what they are doing and offering, the chair is able to stop the typist and edit the action points. During a crisis, maybe the most nerve-wracking job in the room is that of the typist.

But the set-up has been criticised for limiting ministers' access to technology, with not even laptops being allowed in and people reportedly having to resort to illustrating their ideas with pen and paper. COBR is considered the most secure environment for high-level conversations to take place, but that doesn't mean that leaks never occur. When

Dominic Cummings appeared before a select committee looking into the government's response to Covid, he described the briefings as 'Potemkin' and said that whenever he wanted to have conversations he did not want to appear in the media, he chose to have them one-to-one. But despite their dysfunction during Boris Johnson's premiership, they have continued to be of use, with Keir Starmer convening a meet during the Southport riots of 2024 and even Cummings admitting they worked well under Johnson during flooding incidents.

In the secure room, Farage is greeted by Jenkyns, bleary-eyed and wearing a tracksuit, as well as the head of the Environment Agency, the chief executive to the prime minister, the chief of the defence staff and officials from the Civil Contingencies Secretariat (CCS). Responding to criticisms from Cummings and others, by 2030 the Cabinet Office has worked with the security services to develop a secure connection for video calls into the COBR meets. On the screen is the face of a woman Farage doesn't recognise.

One by one, those gathered inform the prime minister that Bristol is facing an unprecedented catastrophe – the sea walls are being overwhelmed and there is imminent risk of widespread property damage or even mass casualties if vulnerable people are not evacuated. 'As we speak,' the official from the CCS says, 'a devastating surge is pummelling low-lying areas. We are particularly concerned about Hinkley Point C'. The world's most expensive power station was gearing up to become fully operational after several delays and a cost of £50 billion. 'We don't know if its sea wall is going to hold up.' There's a flash of panic in the eyes of the men and women around the table: they are looking to the man they trust least in the world for leadership at a moment of national crisis.

The head of the EA informs Farage that David Wimble – a name the prime minister recognises, but only just – had managed to arrange for a train to run in the morning. Farming and flooding were far from his priorities, and while Farage carefully mapped his shadow cabinet ahead of the election, appointing some ministers from the ragtag gang who made it past first-past-the-post had basically been a raffle. But Farage knows that he cannot be seen to ignore the Bristolians in their hour of need. He resolves to go, get some pictures taken with his wellies on and then head home for dinner. He'd go in a helicopter, his entourage could take their chances with the train.

When it's the woman on the screen's turn to speak, she introduces herself as the head of Bristol City Council. She's on the ground working with the Environment Agency to tackle the flood response. She informs the prime minister of the serious danger to life and property and tells him what the Council is doing to help.

'But I would just like to add, Prime Minister, that this is the direct result of your party's climate denialism and your refusal to act on the climate emergency. I'm glad you're coming to Bristol tomorrow to witness first-hand what your policies are doing to this country. Banning renewables, repealing the Climate Change Act and starting fracking will only make what is happening in my city all the more common in the next 50 years …'

'Are you finished?'

'No, I'm certainly not. You are a disgrace, Mr Farage! How dare you show your face in a city you are directly responsible for destroying.'

While she's still speaking, Farage leans over to his aide and orders the council leader to be kicked off the meeting. Her face vanishes from the screen. He turns to the chief of the defence staff, General Sir Richard Knighton, who is wearing full military regalia.

'Thank you for being here at such short notice. We will be needing your full support throughout the crisis. When can your troops deploy in Bristol and how many do you have on stand-by?'

'Zero, sir.'

Farage laughs, but General Knighton is not joking. 'All reservists are being readied in case the Argentines invade the Falklands again, sir. Over the oil, sir,' the soldier says and looks over towards Baroness Jenkyns for support.

'You're telling me we can't defend our sovereign territory from the Argies and pick up some soggy grannies in the Bristol Channel at the same time?'

''Fraid not, sir. We don't have enough troops to do both, sir.'

Farage is now in an impossible bind: he can't leave the Falklands undefended in the face of Argentine aggression. Maggie would be turning in her grave. On the other hand, though they may all be hippies, British citizens are being swept away in a deadly storm surge in Bristol. The city voted against him at the election, though, and every single one of its seats has gone Green, so there's hardly any votes to be lost there. But if he sacrifices the Falklands to Milei and loses the oil revenue, Reform voters would surely never forgive him.

'You'll have to manage on your own then for now,' Farage tells the head of the EA.

An official in No 10 approaches him afterwards and tells him that following the COBR meeting, the EA has reached out and requested emergency funds for Bristol.

'We can't afford to endorse them too much,' Farage says, sensing a political opportunity. 'They'll have to survive with what they've got.'

9 a.m.

Farage, who it is said reads almost every newspaper every morning and has done for nearly his whole life, only has time to flick through them today in the helicopter on the way to the West Country. The *Guardian* somehow has a full dispatch from the morning's COBR meeting: 'Bristol Council Chief Kicked From Floods Crisis Zoom' runs the headline. The *Telegraph* has gone for 'Quango Chief Refused Extra Cash As Floods Devastate Bristol'. *The Times* has picked out the military line: 'Falklands Invasion Scare As Army Chief Diverts Troops From Bristol Catastrophe'.

There was only one image on every front page: an aerial shot of thousands of brand-new cars scattered across the Bristol Channel after the storm surge had descended on to one of Britain's largest new-car storage points at Avonmouth. At its peak, the site has space for 90,000 cars: thousands were now bobbing around in the choppy waters, an atoll of red, blue and white in a sea of brown. There were many scenes of devastation for picture editors to choose from: millions of trees had come down overnight, medieval bridges as far away as the Somerset Levels had collapsed and ancient parish churches were swamped up to shoulder height. Bristol's steep northern escarpment meant that water was funnelled into the city centre and was prevented from spreading out, resulting in flood depths several metres higher than anyone had predicted. The areas spared from the sitting flood water appeared like a moonscape, with whole sections of road torn up by the force of the surge and debris scattered everywhere. Bloated corpses of livestock covered fields. In the city centre, rescue dinghies zipped between an archipelago of office blocks, while a BBC helicopter captured the scene at Ashton Gate Stadium, home to Bristol City FC, which rises out of the surrounding lagoon that is Bedminster.

Perhaps the most striking image of all, however, was the destruction of SS *Great Britain*, the largest ship in the world in the mid-nineteenth century, powered by steam and designed by Isambard Kingdom Brunel. It is the pride of Bristol, designed and built in the city by the legendary engineer who forged the Great Western Railway line to London. When the surge hit at 4 a.m., it flooded the ship's dry dock, tearing the vessel from its secure chains and tipping it on to its side. The impact had snapped the mast and shattered the hull. A crowdfunding campaign to fix its hull already had £15,000 in donations.

There was one sliver of good news. The sea wall at Hinkley had held, and a nuclear disaster had been averted. But there was chaos at Seabank power station and tens of thousands of residents were without power. The fact that Bristol had not become the next Fukushima was of little comfort.

Farage's advisors, despite continual warnings from officials, had got on the train to Bristol to show loyalty to Farage, only to be evacuated by emergency services outside Keynsham. Jenkyns had stayed in London: she had the excuse of important meetings to do with the GCRB. The first thing Farage's entourage notice when they are rescued is the stench. One person involved in flood response in 2025 says: 'It stinks. It really smells because the flood water going through people's houses is contaminated by sewage. You go when the flood waters recede and you can see toilet roll stuck on the roads because it's obviously mixed in with everything from the sewers.'

Bristolians boo the prime minister as his helicopter lands on a rooftop and his vessel negotiates the waterways: it passes over the submerged Redcliffe Way and into the harbour, now indistinguishable from the rest of the city centre. There's a crowd of people waiting for Farage as his boat moors below the cathedral. 'WHERE ARE THE ARMY?' one of the placards reads. He is marched to a briefing, where he is told that at least four people have died overnight and at least two others are missing. Two of the dead are 17-year-olds who had been swept into a storm drain while walking home in Avonmouth.

It still hasn't stopped raining.

11 a.m.

A Planet Justice activist takes the microphone under a gazebo set up on College Green outside the room where Farage, his advisors and Wimble are being briefed. 'Bristol. We were warned of the disastrous impact a major flood would have within the next 40 years.[21] Last night, our city was vandalised not by nature, but by an abuse of nature at the hands of the people inside that building. The prime minister, his environment secretary David Wimble, and his energy secretary, Andrea Jenkyns, hang your heads in shame.' The activist leads calls of 'shame' as the drum beats grow louder. Richard Tice, watching events unfold live on the TV in No 11, felt relieved he'd decided not to take on the Energy brief.

As Wimble comes out of the city hall, someone tries to throw a milkshake at him but misses. He is caught on camera putting his middle finger up at protesters, who crowd around his car as it speeds off to a hotel in Clifton. An event in the cathedral is cancelled after the bishop refuses to allow the prime minister to speak to the congregants at a vigil for the dead. The other two people who were killed were two black men in one of Bristol's poorest neighbourhoods. The Bishop of Bristol pays tribute to them in her homily that evening: 'I knew the mothers of these beautiful men. I christened them as babies. This flood has exposed the inequalities of class and race which have seeped into every crevice of the politics of this city. Like the flood water, it stinks: the prime minister should take a long look at his soul and act with humility as he meets our stricken fellow citizens.'

Instead of attending the service, Farage heads to an affected pub to meet a landlord, whose cellars are underwater and his

---

[21] A McKinsey report in April 2020 predicted that a once-in-200-years flood in 2065 would cause 20 per cent of the city centre to be flooded, with urban areas under an average of 1.4m of water. It said such a catastrophe would cause between $160 and $240 million of damage to real estate, with between $500 and $2,800 million knock-on effects from lost working hours and blackouts.

casks ruined. But when the prime minister arrives on a speedboat, the landlord locks the doors and shouts at him from a window in an upstairs room, where he is sheltering. The moment is caught for the cameras: 'Get away from my pub! You ruined my pub! Don't come to me for a photo opportunity!'

The landlord then chucks a bucket of dirty water at Farage from the window. The clip goes viral on local Facebook groups, and in an interview with BBC Points West, the publican threatens legal action against the government. 'They said in 2019 they wanted to build us a Thames Barrier for Bristol, nothing happened,' he says in a thick West Country accent. 'They spent nearly £7 million on flood defences in Avonmouth. It wasn't finished in time – fat lot of good that money did! Four people have died. They cut the people who could have actually helped us out of this mess. And now we learn that instead of deploying troops to help us down here, he's trying to resurrect Maggie's ghost for a war in the Falklands. It's madness. We didn't vote for these tossers in Bristol and we don't want him here.'

Meanwhile, Dominic Cummings is giving his first interview after he stormed out of Downing Street with his cardboard box three weeks ago. After months of in-fighting, he had been fired for negatively briefing against the prime minister. The final straw was a Cabinet meeting during which Farage pointedly asked why Cummings' beloved scientific research unit ARIA (Advanced Research + Invention Agency), which by 2029 was receiving tax-payer funded grants to the tune of £350 million a year, should be exempt from Reform's efficiency drive.

When asked by a GB News reporter, who has tracked him down to his wife's family home, Chillingham Castle, what he thinks of the government's response to the floods in Bristol, Cummings replies: 'Fucking inept, but I'm not surprised. Some of the team are coke-heads, others are morons. Coke-heads and morons fall apart under pressure.'

4 p.m.

Farage decides to call off the tour and head back to dry land to record a video.

'What I have seen today in one of our greatest cities has shocked me. My sympathies go out to all the families who are dealing with flooded homes across Bristol and Somerset, and to the families of the four people who have tragically lost their lives, and the missing.

'But the stories I've been told down here about the mismanagement by the Environment Agency are an absolute disgrace. The way they have left this city undefended has resulted in this utter shambles. Councillors suggested a Thames Barrier-style project in 2019. What happened to it? They were too busy raising the trans flag and filling diversity quotas to notice the catastrophe that was waiting to happen. They prioritised woke "natural" flood defences like beaver dams in rivers over the lives of their own voters. They put beavers first, not human beings. I have been informed today that several key flood barriers were left open due to late-running works on the Avonmouth barrier. Too busy calling me a racist and wasting money on green crap. I am today calling on the head of the Environment Agency and the head of Bristol City Council to resign with immediate effect. The pair have left our nation, sadly, looking weak on the world stage. I'm not surprised that a poll today shows that the majority of people in this country think the Environment Agency has done a very bad job.'

4.30 p.m.

Meanwhile, Carla Denyer, the Green MP in the centre of the city and therefore in one of the worst-affected areas, is out working with members of the Local Resilience Forum, saving families with children and old people from their homes. 'The MP has won praise for joining a volunteer force on night duties attempting to rescue as many people as she can,' the GB News reporter on the scene told viewers. His words were accompanied by pictures of Denyer walking through brown water in waders with a drenched spaniel in her arms; drinking a cup of tea from a flask in the flooded front room of an elderly woman, where the flood line showed water had risen to over the mantelpiece; and Denyer addressing angry Bristolians on College Green and calling for a vote of no confidence in the government.

Joining her is Dale Vince, the clean energy entrepreneur, former Labour donor, and Green MP for nearby Stroud, as well as members of Bristol band Massive Attack, who say that they will personally pay for thousands of sandbags and bottles of fresh water for communities across the city. Vince says he has, on the request of Polanski, donated his electric-powered speedboat to the rescue attempts.

'In this notebook,' Denyer tells the crowd, 'I have made a list of every request and demand made of me and listened to how Nigel Farage and this Reform government have failed you. We will never forget what happened last night. This crisis is not just a climate emergency, it's a housing emergency, a class emergency, a racism emergency, a gender emergency. We know that in Bristol, but the prime minister, who parachuted into this city this morning, hates us and what we stand for.'

5 p.m.

At the Department of Energy, Andrea Jenkyns is on the phone to a renewable energy boss, making one last-ditch effort to save her energy agenda. 'We'll shut you off from the UK energy market. You won't have any involvement in future, unless you make a deal to leave our markets,' she says. She had finally conceded with her officials that cancelling contracts unilaterally would lead to higher bills and a litany of legal fights. Her review into increasing Britain's gas fleet had ended in failure too: they were astronomically expensive, took five years to build and manufacturers were winding down production as the rest of the world went renewable. 'Name your price,' she shouts at the mild-mannered Dane on the other end of the phone. The next moment, the line goes dead.

6 p.m.

Farage asks his driver to stop beside the Clifton Suspension Bridge so he can have a smoke. He is very rarely alone now he's prime minister. The Avon is so high, the grandeur of Brunel's sweeping wrought-iron design is much diminished. His mobile rings.

'Prime Minister, I've just seen on the TV that terrible incident with the bucket and the publican,' the voice said. It was Lord Bamford, the JCB tycoon who had switched from the Conservatives to become a Reform peer at the election. In 2025, he donated £200,000 to the Party ahead of the local elections in May 2026.

'Where are you staying tonight?'

The prime minister names the miserable three-star B&B Downing Street has booked for him. All the usual options were underwater.

'You can't be stuck there all week with that Denyer woman on the march. Where are you? I'll send over my chopper to Clifton Downs and we can pick you up and you can come and stay here in the Cotswolds. How about that? How does a night at Daylesford sound?'

It's quite normal for politicians to get into difficulties while visiting flood zones and Farage admits he is stuck. Emma Hardy, Labour's floods minister, got stranded in Peterborough when floods hit in early 2024. There were no trains, her taxi left her in the pouring rain and she was only rescued by an Environment Agency worker who managed to get to an unaffected station. Unlike Hardy, there's no getting home for David Wimble, who Farage orders to stay on the ground to manage the rest of the fallout.

Half an hour later, Farage is flying above the deluge when he gets a text: The President of the United States is on the line and wants to speak when you land in the Cotswolds.

11 p.m.

'Hello, Mr President. You've caught me in the Cotswolds this evening, I've just been visiting the floods in Bristol,' the prime minister says.

'The Cotswolds are beautiful, I hope they haven't been affected at all,' JD Vance replies.

'No, no, just Bristol. You know what these things are like, it's always our fault.'

The president, it is soon clear, has a bone to pick with the prime minister. They were friends, but things have got out of hand. He says that he has just got off the phone with the US ambassador in London and has also had the Argentine president in the Oval Office earlier in the day.

'He says you want war over this drop of oil in the Falklands. This is not the 1980s, Nigel, and we both know that you're not capable of defending Port Stanley. I will tell you now that the US will not be supporting any action you take, and if you do so, we will make life very difficult for your troops. You can't do this without us.'

Farage tries to butt in, but the president cuts him off: 'I don't care if you want the oil. I can't have a war in the South Atlantic right now, understand?'

The next day, Farage orders the chief of the defence staff to stand down. 'It ranks as the most humiliating day for British foreign policy since the loss of the Suez Canal,' *The Times*' leader concludes. 'The sight of a prime minister frittering away the country's military and diplomatic reputation on the global stage, while one of its most important cities lies underwater, is a grave blow to our standing.'

In punishment, JD Vance recognises the Falkland Islands as Islas Malvinas. President Milei celebrates by chainsawing an effigy of the British prime minister from a balcony in Buenos Aires, and a single Argentine flag was seen to fly over the roof of Bristol City Hall.

5
Be Objective

FIVE MONTHS EARLIER

Saturday, 6 October 2029, 11 p.m.

At the prime minister's reception for Reform MPs at Chequers no one wants to talk about the BBC. The broadcaster had proved to be a thorn in the side of the fledgling Farage administration ever since the election. The director general's pick for political editor had already, in the government's first three months, broken a series of stories exposing scandals among the parliamentary party: there was the MP who had asked questions at the Foreign Affairs Select Committee on behalf of China after being blackmailed over his teenage membership of the Communist Party and a leaked recording of an advisor boasting about having made millions betting on big falls in the share price of British-based housebuilders and retailers during market uncertainty just after the election; the stories had left the party feeling under fire.

Farage is shocked when, over whiskies and cigars late in the evening, he is taken aside by a handful of MPs wearing furrowed brows, who tell him that if he doesn't get a grip on his party, then they would vote against his Great Repeal Bill (GRB) – 'It's nothing personal, Nige, but no human beings should be treated like that. The Bill needs more protections.' With a majority of only 20, he has no choice but to listen.

WHAT IF REFORM WINS

Monday, 8 October 2029, 9 a.m.

Back in Downing Street, Farage holds an urgent meeting with his closest advisors and whips. They need something to galvanise the Party and see off the threat to the GRB. There is only one possible course of action: whack the BBC.

Wednesday, 10 October 2029, 8 p.m.

The director general of the BBC glances down at the unknown number calling him as he attends the private view of the National Gallery's Francisco Goya exhibition. He ducks into the foyer as a series of other grey-haired notables filter past.

'Hello, Richard Tice here,' the voice on the other end of the line declares.

A call from the chancellor was rarely good news. When George Osborne entered the Treasury in 2010, he was 'somewhat shocked' at the power it had over the national broadcaster: 'You think of the BBC as being this big, independent organisation with lots of protection against the government of the day, even if they have rows about a particular programme. But the chancellor can basically boss the BBC around on its finances,' he said in 2024.

The Treasury sets the TV licence fee and can decide at any point to change or cut it. 'There is nothing to stop a government deciding to revoke the licence fee agreement. As soon as a new government came into office it could, if it chose, regard the licence fee as simply another financial matter which the chancellor could deal with,' one BBC executive said. 'There is very little security in the licence fee.' The other two levers the government has over the broadcaster are negotiating the Royal Charter, which at the time of writing will last for a decade from 2027, and appointing the BBC's chair, deputy chair and board member for England. The members representing Scotland, Wales and Northern Ireland are chosen with input from the devolved national governments. All the other nine board members are appointed internally.

Ripping up the Royal Charter requires an Act of Parliament and a signature from the King, which will take time, as would replacing individual board members. But it's not impossible. The licence fee, which makes up 65 per cent of the BBC's income, however, is its Achilles heel. In 2010, Osborne threatened to cut it if bosses didn't agree to funding the World Service mostly themselves, and gave the BBC less than a week to agree before he was to announce the deal in a speech anyway. The situation for the broadcaster is made worse by the fact its ability to borrow money to finance itself through periods of instability is restricted by the government.

In 2029, the BBC continues to flounder. Fewer than 21 million people are paying for the licence fee for the first time, leading to dramatically falling revenues; young people continue to turn to YouTube, piracy and the streaming giants instead of the national broadcaster; there's been a spike in licence fee evasion and a new scandal rocks the organisation every few months about a highly-paid star's behaviour. The latest meltdown came when Claudia Winkleman called Farage a 'fascist' on her private Instagram account after his immigration speech outside Downing Street. The post was swiftly deleted but the damage had been done: the *Mail*'s front page inevitably screams 'TRAITOR!' There's a sense of constant embattlement.

As its executives like to say: 'You're only as popular as your last *Panorama*'. But the election of Reform in June 2029 was the biggest crisis yet. Reform had made it a manifesto commitment to 'abolish' the licence fee and turn the BBC into a subscription service in the years following the 2024 election, but when Richard Tice enters the Treasury, he is told, like many chancellors before him, that the pledge would be 'extremely brave' to put into practice. Even in 2040, it is predicted some 5 per cent of people in Britain will not be connected to internet-enabled TVs. Officials tell Tice he would effectively be telling those people that the BBC will be forcibly taken from them unless they pay for a monthly broadband subscription, as well as a separate charge for the content. Tice's special advisor points out that many are Reform voters and it would be best not to anger them. But now, the chancellor has finally had the order from Downing Street. It's time to fire the starting gun on licence fee negotiations. He informs the director general that they are already drafting the letter informing him that they will cut the licence fee by 50 per cent this year, with the long-term intention to move the BBC on to a subscription model. Cuts of this scale are not unknown – in 2025, the amount of public money the BBC received was reduced by 30 per cent over 15 years.

'But what about a negotiation?' the DG begins.

'This has come directly from the prime minister. Come to No 11 on Monday.'

The line goes dead. Such negotiating tactics over the licence fee are common at the highest levels: in 2010, the then DG Mark Thompson was called back from his commute home to Oxford at the last minute to engage in late-night negotiations at the Department for Culture, Media and Sport (DCMS) to prevent the broadcaster from agreeing to shoulder the cost of free licences for the over-75s. George Osborne later said that Thompson missed a trick in not being quicker to play off the coalition partners against each other. But that was just with the Tories and Liberal Democrats. One of the easiest things Reform could do was simply to cut the £100 million grant which the Foreign Office gives the World Service each year. The other is local radio, which could be closed down as quickly as it takes to sack staff and pay redundancy. This time the DG has no idea what to expect.

The next morning, he orders his team to draw up a list of popular channels, programmes and stars that would have to be lost if Tice's plans went through. These threats are the weapons with which the broadcaster has to defend itself. In 2015, during negotiations between the then DG Tony Hall and the Conservative-majority government, Hall proposed shutting down BBC 2, BBC 4, all local radio stations and the national stations of Wales, Scotland and Northern Ireland in the face of cuts. David Cameron personally intervened to pull back on some proposals, wary of expending too much political capital on a bruising fight with the beloved national broadcaster. Relations deteriorated further under Boris Johnson, when Dominic Cummings allegedly vowed to abolish the licence fee and sell off its stations. This would have required legislation in Parliament, but the plans never made it beyond the newspapers.

Friday, 12 October 2029, 10 a.m.

Negotiations over the Charter renewal and the licence fee are meant to happen on three levels: first, DCMS officials and BBC staff argue line by line about details: in 2025 two or three civil servants had been working on the BBC's 2027 Charter for over a year, and had spoken to at least 200 people including experts, industry heads, politicians and BBC bosses to get their views on what should change in the next settlement. Then the culture secretary and director general meet to discuss outstanding issues. Finally, the DG is summoned to Downing Street to iron out the last disagreements. In 2029, Farage and Tice summon the DG and chairman to No 10 straight away.

The DG begins by laying out what he would have to do to balance the budgets if the BBC were to make cuts at the level proposed: 'We would have to cancel *Strictly* and wind down BBC 2, and stop covering national sporting events like Wimbledon and the World Cup. Everything would go except for our core offering of BBC 1 and covering the key national occasions like royal weddings, elections and important funerals. It would be the end of the BBC as we know it.'

Cancelling *Strictly* would make Reform unpopular, but it would also cripple the Corporation: the more popular the programme, the more likely people who regularly watch TV would pay their licence fee. 'Threatening to cut those things would probably be a bit of an idle threat,' someone familiar with how the negotiations work said. 'A determined government simply wouldn't believe that that is what the BBC would choose to cut.'

'You don't need to do all of those things, it's far too much. Let the streamers do it – they do it better and don't force everyone to pay for it. The licence fee is the most regressive tax in the country. It's taxation without representation,' Farage says.

The culture secretary Nadine Dorries nods away in the corner.

Now it's the chancellor's turn. 'Cut Fiona Bruce's £410,000 salary. Why do you need 60 radio stations? Get rid of BBC Radio 6 and the other channels nobody listens to and focus on what you do well,' he adds. 'The licence fee should reflect the fact that a large number of people are not paying for it. It's important for the BBC to internalise the new thinking under a Reform government. You're not separate from the efficiency agenda.'

Dorries takes her cue. 'The BBC cannot be a special case. We are cutting every government department and as the national broadcaster, you must take your fair share. This is a new era: we've had enough of posh boys telling the rest of the country what to do.'

For the director general, a great fan of Radio 6, this is the final straw. After hours going back and forth in a tiny room in Downing Street, he storms out of proceedings along with the chairman – it was impossible for them to agree to the scale of cuts being proposed.

That night, Farage goes on GB News to defend the government: 'What we've seen this week is all the usual suspects jumping to the defence of the BBC – and it's all the same people who love to hate Reform. It's a complete bloody disgrace ... the BBC has been institutionally biased for decades. I well remember the Wilson report two decades ago that said the BBC was not covering areas like Europe and immigration with any sense of impartiality. We can add to that net zero and the horrors that happened in Israel on October 7th 2023. They come for every conservative figure in the country – look what they've said about me, look what they did to the former American president. It's just ghastly. It's offensive – just like much of the BBC's output. Labour leader after Labour leader has put their man in the BBC, but when a Conservative is chosen, the media has a meltdown. You couldn't invent this stuff, the hypocrisy is shameless. You might have noticed that since 2025, millions of people have stopped paying the licence fee. Polling shows that a majority of people in this country want reform of the BBC. At a time of difficult choices, we are asking the national broadcaster to make some economies, and maintaining it at its current rate is simply not sustainable. We want the BBC to still do everything it is currently doing, but to do it cheaper.'

Though it has significant financial powers over the BBC, the government cannot rule on whether it is upholding impartiality or not. This is the role of the independent regulator Ofcom, but the government does select its board. Viewers must complain to the BBC first, which can then be escalated to Ofcom if the complainant is unhappy. Ofcom can fine the BBC, ask it not to repeat a programme, or issue a correction. For example, in 2025, the BBC was forced by Ofcom to make an on-air apology for failing to disclose that the narrator of a documentary about Gaza was the son of a Hamas official.

Questions have previously been raised about Ofcom's proximity to Downing Street: under Boris Johnson, Theresa May's former director of communications, Sir Robbie Gibb, was asked to run the process for selecting the new Ofcom chair. When Farage casts around for other weapons with which to clobber the broadcaster, he is delighted to discover the vacancy for the chairmanship is due to become available within his first year in office. The prime minister is starting to understand just what damage he can inflict on one of his oldest foes.

Monday, 15 October 2029, 5 p.m.

Sky's owner Comcast Corporation holds a press conference from its headquarters in Philadelphia. In this scenario, the American multinational media company, which runs Sky News in the UK, went ahead with plans suggested first in 2025 and bought ITV for £2 billion three years later.[22] The deal gave Comcast a 40 per cent stake in ITN (Independent Television News), the broadcast company which produces

---

[22] The deal would end ITV's 70 years of independence and leave Channel 4 a comparative minnow in the world of British public service broadcasting by comparison. It would likely lead to calls for Channel 4 and the BBC to merge to ensure its survival. There have been regular calls from Conservative administrations for such an arrangement given the broadcasters' funding problems, and in January 2026 Labour's creative industries minister Ian Murray raised the prospect of a partnership in a letter to Ofcom and the Competition and Markets Authority.

news programmes for ITV, Channel 4 and Channel 5. While each of these channels is independent, ITN makes the editorial decisions. ITN and the broadcasters might choose the presenter of the news programme together, and the broadcasters may make demands of ITN, such as having a certain percentage of its programmes as foreign news, but ITN decides which stories to cover, where to send its outside broadcasts and what words or images are used on the news programmes it makes. Controlling it gives Comcast huge influence over the British media landscape.

'It does not make financial sense for Comcast to keep two loss-making news operations in the same country, so today we announce that we are merging Sky and ITN in the UK,' the company's chief executive Brian Roberts says.

In one stroke of a pen, the tectonic plates of information and democracy in the UK shift. The news programmes of four of the major channels in the UK are now ultimately under the control and direction of an American news corporation.

'ITN will have to honour its existing contract to ITV, but beyond that, it's open season in terms of editorial control,' a media analyst writes in a post on LinkedIn. 'It makes total sense for Sky News to make ITV News now that Comcast has committed to it for the foreseeable future.'

Comcast, a company little-known in the UK, has shown itself willing to bend the knee under political pressure. The company was criticised by some of its own anchors when in 2025 it chose to donate an undisclosed amount along with other big businesses to demolish the East Wing of the White House and build Donald Trump a $300 million ballroom in its place. Critics called it a brazen attempt to win presidential favour and oil the wheels of future dealmaking.

In 2029, Britain is served by a public broadcaster in crisis and an American multinational which has a history of putting its commercial interests ahead of editorial independence. The public's access to reliable information is further eroded by ever-evolving consumer habits: even more so than they had in 2025, people get their news from podcasts, TikTok, tabloid websites and Elon Musk's X, few of which prioritise chasing down stories and holding the government to account.

Three months on from the election, even at GB News the heady events of June and the victory party feel very long ago. The channel had found itself in a difficult position. Farage has had to cancel his weekly show now that he's prime minister and many of its staff took advisory roles with the change of government. Without a government to protest against, viewing figures begin to fall. The channel hires media-savvy hosts of far-right podcasts and YouTube channels, and swings firmly to the far-right. This is part of a wider shift in British politics: driven by the always-online Gen Z right, the Overton Window (the range of views considered acceptable for discussion in mainstream debate) had moved in an unmistakably conservative direction. In the Reform era, Cameron Tories are left-wing, while the Liberal Democrats are socialists.

The editors at GB News are only now starting to capture the old insurgent dynamic again by platforming figures that are ever more extreme in their criticisms of Farage's government. This wins praise from some counterintuitive parts of the press. 'In a world where broadcast news in the UK has come under the control of an American multinational, and the BBC is in crisis over cuts by the chancellor to the licence fee, GB News has emerged as a lone independent voice free to criticise the government,' the *Economist* writes. 'Liberals may hate its line, but its focus on holding the government's feet to the fire is heartening, if unexpected.'

Friday, 19 October 2029, 4 p.m.

In Essex, the trial of the migrant accused of burning down St Anselm's parish hall approaches its conclusion. There is

BE OBJECTIVE

huge media interest in the case: editors send out reporters to knock on doors looking for eye-witnesses and frightened locals, many of whom use the opportunity to complain about the situation at Manston, which is dominating headlines. The migrant is found guilty and a few weeks later, he is sentenced to a year in jail. There is immediate outrage: Reform MPs call for the judge to resign, Justice Secretary Sarah Pochin files an appeal and a group of protesters waving St George flags attempt to ram the truck as the convicted man leaves court.

Press secretaries Ed Sumner and James Gill and new advisor Dan Sambrook watch the chaos play out on someone's phone, out on the Downing Street Rose Garden patio. It's the end of a long week and another unseasonably warm day: ties undone, shoes on the table, cigarettes lit, the pirates are making plans for the weekend. All except Sambrook, who has work to do. He had been drafted in as an advisor in the Policy Unit to help with the Great Repeal Bill after making an impression with his impassioned appearance on the BBC's election day panel and is not quite part of the group yet. The others regard him as a jumped-up influencer who has got into the building on his follower count rather than loyalty. Sambrook is staring at the video over their shoulders.

'He's a savage. He'll be back on the street within six months,' Sambrook says. There's an awkward silence before a few of the junior members of staff laugh politely. 'There'll be a civil war soon, honestly,' Sambrook adds, once the giggling has died down.

Gill and Sumner meet each other's eyes. Downing Street staffers are often suspicious of newcomers: What are his politics? Do we allow him into our plotting? Is he one of us?

'Very robust, Dan,' says Katie, a Policy Unit official.

'I think it's time for us to go home,' Gill says.

'I can stay on to do a statement on this mess,' offers Sambrook.

'No, don't worry. I can handle it. You guys get home and I'll see you Monday.'

Saturday, 20 October 2029, 9 a.m.

With the BBC and Reform locked in a tussle over a cut to the licence fee, news of a threat to the national broadcaster leaks out. There's uproar across the nation. Anger is felt especially among older people, who are far more likely to watch and listen to the BBC. The protest group 38 Degrees organises for a million letters to be sent to the BBC board, objecting to the proposals. The Our BBC group, an offshoot of the Our Rights immigration protest movement, holds a march of thousands down Regent's Street past Broadcasting House in protest at the changes. Green leader Zack Polanski on the BBC's *Question Time* goes viral with a rant about the attempt to 'abolish' the BBC and silence journalism.

'It's the only time I can think of when a group of people have ever marched down Whitehall to pay more money for something,' one Reform MP quips on an LBC discussion panel.

10 a.m.

Dan Sambrook packs his car and, with his children, drives to his parents' home in Folkestone, Kent. He leaves the kids with their grandparents for the day while he hunkers down in his old box room, now a storeroom for the dozens of pieces of camera equipment from his years spent filming small boats on the beaches.

He begins on a note for the prime minister entitled 'Beyond the Great Repeal Bill: Proposal to Launch

BE OBJECTIVE

Remigration Strategy'. As an advisor in Downing Street, Sambrook has huge power to shape policy and dictate the political agenda of the Home Office, the department for which he is responsible. Whitehall often refers to Downing Street as the 'Centre' for good reason: power is highly concentrated within its walls and government departments are treated as necessary problems to be solved rather than places where new ideas originate.

'Advisors work for the PM to scrutinise how the departments are doing,' one source explained. 'They are encouraged to come up with ideas that have not come from the department and then persuade [them] or impose [the policy] on them. Departments often come up with policy which aligns with their objectives, but their objectives may not totally match [our] objectives.'

It's a style which suits 'incredibly full of themselves men' comfortable with the atmosphere of machismo prevalent in the modern Downing Street, which has led some in Labour to brand No 10 a 'boys' club' since 2024.

In 2029, thinking about the methods of the previous administration was like trying to imagine a highly sophisticated ancient society which had been swept away by a great flood. In the Downing Street of 2025, Sambrook was told, an array of bureaucratic hoops had to be jumped through to get policy proposals before Keir Starmer. Special advisors initiated and generated the majority of submissions, or 'subs', and worked with officials in the Policy Unit to agree on recommendations. The draft document was then seen by all the different relevant teams within Downing Street, including communications, who contributed their considerations. It then received sign-off from the head of the Policy Unit, before being handed to the prime minister's inner circle, known as the 'outer office' – so-called because you have to pass where they sit to reach the PM's office. This included former Chief of Staff Morgan McSweeney and his then deputies, Vidhya Alakeson and Jill Cuthbertson, and the principal private secretary (PPS), Dan York-Smith. Outer office had the opportunity to add a note for the prime minister, which was not seen by the advisor.

Few processes from Starmer's Downing Street remain now. A slew of senior civil servants had left, only to be replaced with officials chosen for their politics rather than their ability. Outer office remains, an institutional coccyx made up of Dominic Cummings; 'Posh' George Cottrell, who still doesn't have an official role, and Dan Jukes, Director of Communications. The Policy Unit on the second floor is staffed entirely by 10DS and the Reform Research Department, an outfit which Dan Sambrook's old friends at the *Pimlico Journal* regard as something of a joke. 'The whole operation is ridiculously short-termist, reactionary and amateur,' Sambrook had complained to a journalist over a pint, a week earlier. He hopes the plans he is working on in his childhood bedroom will jolt the others into thinking about something more ambitious.

The beneficiaries of the elaborate procedural architecture in 2025 were the officials in the prime minister's private office: they used their power to mediate who and what the prime minister saw to exert control over policy. The result was sometimes inertia and frustration. Sometimes it could take two weeks for a proposal to wend its way through the channels to get in front of Starmer. This inevitably led to friction between officials and advisors.

With Dominic Cummings, that system was never going to survive. The friction quickly becomes outright hostility, with Cummings and his team of advisors despairing at the length of time proposals take to see the light of day. A key 'blocker' is the PPS, the effective head of the civil servants in Downing Street, who previously had the power to dismiss a submission out of hand and had full oversight of the red box. An email is sent around by Cummings from a new address: 'From now on, policy submissions will be sent to this inbox for review by outer office. We will then pass on the ones we deem important for consideration by Nigel.'

The next day, the PPS resigns, as do four of her loyal private secretaries. They are replaced by favoured members of the Reform youth wing. The stolid Civil Service procedures of the Starmer days evaporate. After the officials who carefully collated and consulted each submission are fired, and Cummings' new inbox system is introduced, Farage is suddenly inundated with shoddily typed briefings and incorrect advice, all crammed into his box by an official who looks like he's on work experience.

The political commentator Sam Freedman in his Substack compares the Farage Downing Street to that of Gordon Brown, arguing that internal chaos and disorganisation is not necessarily unheard of at the centre of political power: 'In the New Labour era, Gordon Brown did away with the red box system entirely and select advisors could send notes to an email inbox for him to review and he'd fire back terse replies,' he notes. 'But the dysfunction in the process from what people are telling me is off the charts'.

In most departments of Whitehall in 2025, the red box long ago had become a digital OneNote drive in which secretaries of state could work through submissions digitally, giving comments or asking questions of their advisors and private office. But in No 10 in 2025, it worked differently: Starmer still used the traditional dispatch box, which prime ministers have used in some form since at least the 1860s, and everything he needed was printed on to paper. Advisors handed in their submissions digitally, but they were then laboriously printed off by 'PM Post', the team of secretaries who follow the prime minister everywhere and are responsible for collating documents in the box.

Despite the service, staffers say Starmer was irritated to learn that the iPad he used in Opposition was no longer permitted by Security. He was forced to 'scribble' on a sheet of paper to make his decision known. Farage is more than happy to continue the tradition of the red box and is seen in nearly every one of his TikTok updates posing with it as he signs orders and considers plans for the camera.

Given the importance of his role, many would think the prime minister's red box would be overflowing with decisions which need his input: in fact, Starmer's box was 'tiny' compared to those of his secretaries of state and on his request, policy submissions were mostly kept to three pages, or up to six or seven if it was a very complicated issue. The most diligent secretaries of state might read 'subs' of 20 pages or more, while others hardly read them at all. Grant Shapps was infamous among civil servants for refusing to read anything longer than two sides of A4.

Monday, 22 October 2029, 1 p.m.

In Downing Street, Dan Sambrook lunches with Katie, whom he knows shares his views. That afternoon, she begins working on the details of the policy and uses the phrase 'named list only' when emailing other officials: this keeps the number of eyes on the plans to only those on the list. It's marked 'Official Sensitive: No 10 only'. On the top left is the Downing Street watermark. She returns it to Sambrook, who writes a couple of introductory paragraphs before giving it to one of the new private secretaries to put in Farage's box.

7 p.m.

Dan Jukes is one of Farage's most loyal pirates. He has been by the leader's side since he was 19, when Farage was merely a member of the European Parliament. He orchestrated Farage's victory over Coutts Bank[23] and masterminded his election victory. It is uncommon for the director of communications in Downing Street to be honoured with a seat in outer office and Jukes takes his responsibility seriously. Every night, before Farage goes upstairs, he sifts through his red box to get an understanding of what policies are being fed to the boss.

This evening, amid the scraps of printed-off emails and tea-stained submissions, he spots the word 'remigration' poking up from one of the files. He knows exactly what this means and immediately reaches inside and removes it. Jukes grabs his laptop, and using his outer office access, finds the folder in the Downing Street system. It had been submitted by Dan Sambrook a couple of hours before. He writes a note saying 'WITHDRAWN' beside the submission indicating that it has not been shown to the prime minister and has been removed from his red box. He makes sure to take a screenshot of what he's done, just in case.

Thursday, 24 October 2029, 7.45 p.m.

Camilla,[24] a former Conservative special advisor, arrives at a dinner party hosted by an old colleague in Belsize Park, north London, and hasn't even closed her umbrella when her boyfriend pulls her into a conversation.

'Look what Sophie has on her phone,' he says.

It takes Camilla a minute to register who she is looking at: the back of a familiar figure sitting a laptop in No 10.

---

[23]In 2023, the private bank closed his account after it claimed Farage did not meet its requirement to hold £1 million or more in his account. After a controversy, it emerged the bank had acted in part because of concerns about Farage's political views. The CEO of Coutts' owner NatWest was forced to resign.

[24]The characters in this section are fictional inventions, for illustrative purposes.

'Is that Dan Sambrook? What is this?' she asks. But even before Sophie, who still works in No 10 as a junior official, zooms in, she can read the title in bold: *Beyond the Great Repeal Bill: proposal to launch remigration strategy*. 'Remigration', or the forced mass deportation of foreign-born residents, as the *FT* explainer she had watched a couple of weeks ago had told her. The concept of remigration had started popping up again and again recently: a Reform MP had been criticised after using it in a question at PMQs, an angry member of the *Question Time* audience had been simultaneously booed and cheered for mentioning it in a recent episode, even her teenage brother had started going on about it at dinner on Saturday. In 2025, it was a concept which the vast majority of the country would have defined as pure racism, an idea not even pushed by the likes of Tommy Robinson. In 2029, to much of the public it was an idea that had seemed to appear from nowhere, but those who'd spent time on X and far-right spaces on the internet knew that it had been circulating the mainstream for the last couple of years.

'Dan Sambrook makes some seriously fucking weird comments sometimes. I've overheard him chatting all the time with a colleague of mine – Katie – who adores him. They're working something up about it. I haven't had eyes on it so was really curious. Anyway, I saw this on his computer and thought I'd snap it.'

'Can you send it to me? Can I share it?'

Sophie agrees on the condition of anonymity. Camilla sends a quick message to the BBC's political editor.

7.53 p.m.

A WhatsApp alert pings on the phone of the BBC's political editor, who is still at his desk in the broadcaster's Millbank office late in the evening. He is one of the few to have his own room, but it's a cupboard compared to what he'd have at other organisations. The office is enlivened only by the flicker of a small screen showing a live feed of the Commons. He's with his editor, working through legal objections and impartiality considerations for his latest scoop about a corrupt Reform MP. They haven't said it out loud, but the pair both feel the chilling effect of the government's threat on the licence fee in the newsroom. A few previous stories he had pitched about Farage have been spiked, or if they have been published at all, they mysteriously haven't made it on to the homepage. He has little actual evidence for interference at the level of the newsroom, and his wife thinks he's paranoid.

Impartiality is sacrosanct at the BBC: it's in the first line of its royal charter. Before the election, it felt like an impartial national broadcaster was still sacrosanct for the public too, but the constant scandals and accusations of bias from the prime minister have changed perceptions. Despite the supportive protests at the weekend, a recent poll showed a record jump in the number of people who think the BBC is 'systemically biased'. Since negotiations began, the whole newsroom has felt like it's locked in a constant crouch position. Now, when he's following a big story, more than once an executive has asked: 'Do you really think this is a story? Hasn't the story moved on now?' Among some senior people there's even a growing attitude that the BBC 'shouldn't do news' but instead merely follow the papers and other outlets. 'Protect the institution,' they say.

He thinks of them as he studies the message he has just been sent by Camilla.

8.20 p.m.

'We need to get this up tonight,' the editor of the *News at Ten* programme says, when the political editor shows him what he's got. The political editor is already scrolling to find Dan Sambrook's number to WhatsApp him, requesting a comment. His boss is adding the news line to that evening's list: 'A leaked Downing Street memo seen by the prime minister proposes the mass deportation of foreign-born citizens'. It's almost impossible for a senior member of the BBC's board, or a government minister, to suppress a damaging story if the programme's editor wants it published. The political editor remembers those comments from senior staff and wonders if he would struggle to get the story out if they knew. Those leading the BBC have to make political decisions all the time about how to manage its relationship with government and the country, but according to one former editor, 'if the 99.5 per cent of the staff of the BBC get a whiff of the fact that the 0.5 per cent at the top of the BBC are trying to do a political deal by offering to suppress something, then you can be sure it'll lead the 10 o'clock news.'

The BBC loves nothing more than to navel-gaze at a time of crisis, as the Trump *Panorama* documentary row in 2025 demonstrated: 'BBC News staff feel it incumbent on themselves to bare their chests and frankly dig at their own bosses, and there's nothing they find more professionally or personally satisfying than putting the knife into the DG or the head of news on air if there's some suspicion that the BBC is up to some political skulduggery.' In times of crisis, the broadcaster can be its own worst enemy.

But first, the political editor has to stand it up. This involves interviewing his source so they can confirm to him what they've seen. The BBC has a double-sourcing policy, so he needs one other person to verify the document. He has already confirmed with his first source, Camilla, and so he now sends an email to Dan Sambrook for comment. Immediately, his phone lights up with Sambrook's name.

'You cannot run this, you fucking prick,' Dan rants for a while, before the political editor sends him the picture of the back of his head hunched over the memo at his desk in No 10.

'Who took that?'

'Are you denying it?'

There is silence down the end of the line.

'Has the PM seen it?' asks the political editor.

'Off the record?'

'Yes.'

'Yeah, it went into his red box,' says Sambrook. 'He was subbed on, one of the officials put it in.'

8.31 p.m.

Dan Jukes answers the call from the BBC's political editor from his table at 5 Hertford Street. He makes his apologies to the table of boorish Reform MPs he has been tasked with getting to know.

'What do you want?' Jukes' face drops as the details of the story are read to him. A restless man, he is never able to sit still or leave things alone. He is pacing up and down outside the club and loses his composure when the journalist starts to read out the submission.

'Our sources tell us that this advice has gone all the way up to the prime minister. Do you recognise that?' the political editor asks.

A group of tourists cross the street as Jukes yells down the phone. 'That's fucking bollocks! The PM did not see that sub,' he seethes. 'If you run with that, you'll regret it.'

9.46 p.m.

Dan Jukes leaves dinner and heads back across St James's Park to Downing Street. As he passes a pod of pelicans in the moonlight, an idea suddenly strikes him. He lets himself in via the Horse Guards door. He heads to the comms room on the ground floor, apologises to the cleaner, who is busy at work, and flicks on one of the screens. He rarely watches the 10 o'clock news but this time he thought he'd enjoy it. He refuses a call from the political editor, who texts asking what evidence he has that Farage did not see the memo.

10 p.m.

'BBC News has seen a memo to the prime minister which recommends the mass forced migration of millions of foreign-born citizens from the UK. This programme can reveal that Nigel Farage was presented with documents supporting plans to detain and deport all foreign-born residents under a policy of "remigration", a term common on the far-right …'

The BBC publishes a version of the document transcribed from the photo in an article splashed on the BBC News website. Jukes looks down at his phone as a notification appears. He taps the link and reads through the article, which includes the submission transcribed in full:

Official Sensitive: No 10 only
Beyond the Great Repeal Bill: proposal to launch remigration strategy

Policy issue

When the Great Repeal Bill becomes law and we have left the ECHR, we will have significant legal and operational capabilities to deport up to 1.2 million people and bring net migration down to the thousands. This submission is intended to consider what could lie ahead for Reform's immigration policy.

In 2005, there were 5.6 million foreign-born individuals in Britain. By 2023, this had nearly doubled to 10.3 million. The damage to our culture and country has already been done but we can solve the issues we see on our streets through a policy of removals of foreign-born nationals back to their ancestral homelands. This process is known as 'remigration' and has been championed by Germany's opposition party, the AfD, which proposes funding large-scale removals of Syrian residents who acquired citizenship under Angela Merkel. This policy document outlines how it could be implemented in Britain.

Twenty-five years ago, British society was largely cohesive. Now it is a jigsaw puzzle of competing identities, fragmented across race, religion and culture. We ran on a manifesto slogan of 'Family. Community. Country'. All of those things are at risk if Whites cease to become a majority in Britain, as they are predicted to within 40 years.

This is the ultimate result of the failed liberal project of mass migration, which was forced on Britain since Tony Blair's entry into Downing Street in 1997. His army of human rights barristers and judges has set up a legalistic and bureaucratic regime which Reform has only started to disentangle. The question is what can a Reform government unshackled from the ECHR do about it?

Options

Even before the passing of the GRB, we can start looking at making deals with multiple countries in a number of zones around the world. In Africa, Rwanda is the obvious choice; in Europe, it would be building on our relationship with Albania. In South East Asia, Laos has hinted they would be open to such a deal and we would also need a country in the Middle East. We would pay these four or five countries a small amount to take our removals. Once those deals are in place, we can continue to expand Border Force to begin more removals, targeting the ghettos previously mentioned immediately ...

10.03 p.m.

The night reporter at the *Telegraph* rushes over to the late editor and shows him the breaking story. He slowly puts on his glasses. 'You'd better do that up quickly,' he says.

The night editor crafts a line on the late list and calls the editor-in-chief. As he does so, his counterparts at every other Fleet Street paper are doing the same. Next, he calls the newspaper's political editor, who has seen the article and is trying to stand up the story himself, but has had no luck so far.

'This is big, I'd put it on the front if I was you,' he says.

The editor makes the decision to go ahead with the commission, but attributes it to the BBC. The copy is filed within 15 minutes, and the night editor gives it the once-over as the production editor crafts a completely new front page for the newspaper's second edition. The picture editor is busy putting a photo of Sambrook in the online piece, while the live news editor is composing a push notification which is sent to a million smartphones in seconds. The whole process occurs within four and half minutes of the copy being filed.

Already, there is a horrified reaction from MPs, which the paper greedily feeds into its coverage. 'Farage has been exposed as a Nazi at last,' Your Party's Jeremy Corbyn says. A statement put out by former leaders Gordon Brown, John Major and David Cameron's democracy foundation calls the document the 'Rivers of Blood' memo after Enoch Powell's 1968 speech. 'It is deeply troubling that Farage is allegedly flirting with ideas not even entertained by Powell himself,' the statement reads. Powell raised the idea of 're-emigration' in his speech in Birmingham, but rather than forcing migrants to return home, he advocated for a scheme of 'generous assistance' to aid their departure. In January 2024, there were protests in Germany after senior party figures had attended a meeting with an academic who had called for the 'remigration' of asylum seekers, foreigners with residency rights and 'non-assimilated' citizens. This was the first time the term had been heard by much of the public, to the extent that the BBC had an 'explainer' section on it at the bottom of its online article.

A pastor for Britain's largest evangelical church tells *Newsnight* that the plans are a 'devilish fantasy' and evidence that 'the upper echelons of Reform have been captured by wickedness'. Meanwhile, the Archbishop of Canterbury Sarah Mullady puts out a statement that Reform should remember 'Christian values' of 'kindness' and 'tolerance'.

Jukes is still in No 10, his phone buzzing almost every 12 seconds. He ignores the calls as he composes a WhatsApp message firing Dan Sambrook and an email to the overnight security requesting that his pass be immediately cancelled. Next, he calls the prime minister and suggests he might want to call the director general. Farage barks so loudly down the phone in the upstairs flat that Jukes can hear it from his ground-floor office.

Those who have run the BBC have many stories to tell about the bullying tactics from governments of all stripes. Just before the 1997 election, the soon-to-be campaign director of New Labour – Peter Mandelson – called an editor at the BBC to complain about 'entirely false' allegations made in a *Panorama* documentary about the Labour Party to be aired in the following two weeks. He began charmingly, then said: 'Don't try to tell me that [*Panorama*'s] not going to [publish the allegations], because believe me, I know what's going on in the *Panorama* newsroom more than you or Tony Hall do. I know precisely who is saying what in the *Panorama* office, I know what is planned. It is an outrage and I just want you to know that if that programme were ever to see the light of day, then you can kiss goodbye to a new licence fee and if you have any doubt as to who is going to be in power next year, then I suggest you read the opinion polls and go figure!' The editor and the *Panorama* team carried on regardless of the threat.

Jukes rallies the pirates to bombard the BBC's director of news and chair with calls. Even in 2025, under a government which was supposedly friendly to the broadcaster, the culture secretary Lisa Nandy wasn't scared to lift the phone to the BBC whenever a scandal was brewing, insiders said. 'It suggests she's not very experienced in office,' said another BBC source. 'It's her first ministerial role. She really should know that she doesn't lift up the phone to the editor-in-chief of the BBC every time there's something which is causing her a political problem,' they said. The concept of a completely independent BBC has always been a fiction, and Reform are happy to take this to its logical conclusions.

In 2029, Farage slams down the phone to the DG. Meanwhile, Jukes sends a statement to the on-call private office press secretary to distribute: 'The BBC's report is false. The prime minister has never seen this document. The individual responsible for writing it has been sacked.'

Wednesday, 31 October 2029, 12 p.m.

Farage stands at the dispatch box, flanked by his front bench, and faces the Labour opposition at PMQs. MP after

MP stands to denounce the prime minister and his party as racists: 'Gordon Brown was right to call this the "Rivers of Blood" memo. Not since the days of Enoch Powell have politics been so covered in the stench of racism and bigotry,' Labour MP Dawn Butler tells the Commons to cheers from Opposition benches.

Farage waits for the Speaker to bring calm and begins: 'The BBC report aired last week, containing allegations that I received a proposal for mass deportations of people who have a right to work and live in this country, is shocking. I am disgusted and utterly horrified that anyone in Downing Street could have cooked up such a vile policy. That person was immediately dismissed and his Reform membership terminated. Good riddance!'

There was a hum of agreement from loyal Reform MPs.

'For what it's worth, I think it's clear as day what has happened here. It's an establishment stitch-up! It's an irrefutable case of establishment BBC bias against Reform, against me, against the work we are doing to rebuild broken Britain. This is the liberal deep state lashing out as it has done many times before against a person they deem unacceptable. I've said it many times: no one has done more than I to diminish the influence of the far-right in this country. I was responsible for destroying the BNP with UKIP. It's a word I hadn't even heard of until yesterday. Remigration is not and never will be Reform policy. Does this House seriously think that it's a coincidence that this memo surfaces now and is splashed all over the BBC? When the government is locked in negotiations over the licence fee? Come on!

'The BBC has exposed itself for what it is: as soon as anyone dares to question its role, question its ridiculous licence fee, question its board, they turn to smear tactics and establishment bullying. Today I have submitted a complaint to the BBC and I urge the public to do so too.'

Butler stands in a point of order and asks the prime minister directly whether he was ever presented with the document.

'I categorically deny ever reading or seeing this document and refute the BBC's allegation that I was advised on it. It's a farce.'

Later that day, opposition MPs apply to table a motion for a debate on whether Farage should be referred to the Parliamentary Privileges Committee to investigate whether he lied to the House over his knowledge of the submission.

Over the course of the week such is the anger and embarrassment among Reform MPs that some briefed to journalists about how there were '20 to 30' willing to vote against the government and potentially bring down Farage, which could leave him open to a vote of no confidence. MPs are also starting to receive letters from their constituents about the impact of cuts the BBC is beginning to make, especially local radio. Most MPs never feature on network TV or radio, but they appear regularly on England's 38 local radio stations. It looks as though Farage's gamble to unite the Party has put everything at risk and that the memo could topple his government after just 124 days. But when the motion is tabled, Reform whips are ordered by Downing Street to allow the motion to pass.

Farage appears in a video posted to the Downing Street X account: 'Today, I welcomed the Opposition's challenge to investigate me over my knowledge of the remigration memo. I welcome the inquiry and hope they come to a conclusion swiftly.'

Monday, 19 November 2029, 2.30 p.m.

'Boris Johnson called you a kangaroo court and he was right for once!' Farage tells MPs as they grill him during the Privileges Committee hearing. Meanwhile, Dan Jukes and his team unearth previous statements made by hearing members about the memo to discredit them and leak them to the press. He is hauled in front of the committee too, where he produces the screenshot of the Downing Street log showing that he deleted the memo before Farage took his red box that evening. He points to Dan Sambrook as the guilty party, who he accuses of a 'salacious attempt to slander the good name of the PM', and says whoever leaked the memo did so for political purposes. The Committee, following this evidence, find that the prime minister is innocent of misleading the House.

That night, in the kitsch surroundings of the Raffles Old War Office Hotel on Whitehall, Farage hosts a huge celebration paid for by a prominent new donor to the Party. He had wanted it to be in Downing Street but the donor paying for it all was not cleared by Security at the building. The room is decked out to look like a German beer hall, with blonde waitresses in lederhosen serving steins of beer to the Parliamentary Reform Party, favoured journalists, advisors and Tufton Street fellows. Robert Jenrick and Danny Kruger pose with their bratwursts for the cameras as they take seats beside Farage on the high table.

Someone has made facemasks of Dawn Butler and Enoch Powell and passes them around the event. Farage enters the room to roaring applause, sparklers spraying as he mounts the stage.

'They tried to whack us, they tried to divide us. They tried to say we were a bunch of misfits and weirdos. Well, Mr Director General, we're going to whack you right back!' Farage yells. The Party, many of whom are yet to even meet their leader in person, are more united than ever.

As Farage celebrates, the BBC is tearing itself apart as it launches its own investigation into the scandal. After

Farage's statement in the Commons, its internal Executive Complaints Unit was deluged with notices from the public. The unit, which is made up of BBC staff, reviews the thousands of entries. On the BBC's Corrections and Clarifications page, the broadcaster posts a notice:

> We would like to apologise unreservedly to the Prime Minister for a recent report which alleged that he saw a submission now known as the 'Rivers of Blood' memo. We accept that our reporting unintentionally created the impression that the Prime Minister was considering implementing the proposals when instead it was an advisor acting independently. We apologise for this error of judgement.

In a further statement, the director general says he has come to the decision to resign with immediate effect due to a failure of editorial oversight.

News staff break cover and go on the record to newspapers and on social media defending the political editor and calling Farage a fascist. The public appearance of impartiality towards the broadcaster is fracturing by the hour.

Tuesday, 20 November 2029, 2 p.m.

The prime minister puts in a call to a Radio 5 Live phone-in to express his displeasure at the DG's statement. The normal communications 'gridding' process which gives slots to ministers for particular announcements on particular days has broken down in this scenario, with Farage often choosing to intervene at a whim. 'The accusations made in the BBC's original report are so inaccurate and disgusting, and are of such gravity, that they are the clearest evidence yet that the BBC is institutionally biased against me. What more sign can you want? I've been saying this for weeks: it's good the BBC have issued their statement apologising today, but it should have been immediate. Today I will write to the chair of Ofcom to request an investigation into whether there is a broader problem of bias within the BBC. I am content that the DG has done the right thing and resigned, but the rot goes much further than one individual. I will also be instructing lawyers to submit papers as I have been advised I have excellent grounds for a defamation case.'

Meanwhile, rumours circulate that the political editor has had a breakdown and been put on sick leave. His boss, the director of news, is also off. A BBC insider conceded there would have to be 'brutal' conversations in such a scenario.

Monday, 7 January 2030, 9 a.m.

Ofcom releases its ruling on the BBC's reporting on the 'Rivers of Blood' memo. It reveals it has received more than 10,000 complaints from members of the public over the BBC's reporting. In its summary, the regulator said the broadcaster had broken the Broadcasting Code by misleading audiences in a factual broadcast by misreporting the prime minister's knowledge of a submission from a Downing Street advisor. It finds that associating the prime minister with such remarks when he had no knowledge of them amounts to a breach of impartiality, especially given the prominence with which they were reported.

'Trust is at the heart of the relationship between a broadcaster and its audience, particularly for a public service broadcaster such as the BBC. This failing had the potential to erode the significantly high levels of trust that audiences

WHAT IF REFORM WINS

would have placed in BBC factual reporting about the immigration policy of the government.'

3 p.m.

At BBC Millbank, it's quieter than usual, even though political commentators are expecting a showdown over the Great Repeal Bill in the House of Commons the following week. More staff are working from home and most of the new stories on the homepage are follows from the papers.

An article in the *Guardian* from the media correspondent paints a bleak picture of life inside the institution: 'As this episode shows, within the BBC behemoth it is hard to suppress a story. Even though it was incorrect in significant ways, the "Rivers of Blood" memo story did highlight Dan Sambrook's views and position in the Downing Street operation. But where government influence really comes to bear on the BBC is pressure on editors and reporters to not follow up the story, not pushing for the next line, not holding the government accountable. Sources inside the newsroom say multiple board members demanded a meeting with the director of news, who I believe is on sick leave, as they wanted to challenge her over the "damage done" by the story's publication.'

In 2025, BBC journalists were sometimes able to fend off overreach by the board, but by 2029, this has become impossible. The threat of the licence fee cut, and now the huge public embarrassment of this latest fiasco, has left Farage in a more powerful position over the national broadcaster than he could ever have imagined.

The Comcast-owned ITN broadcasters are mysteriously lacklustre in following up damaging details about the memo. Farage had got James Orr to give the US president a call to see what deals could be dangled in front of Comcast's CEO to make sure they fell into line. There are not even questions asked as to the strength of the evidence supplied at the committee hearing by Dan Jukes. What is left of the independent press are denied questions at press conferences. 'Will you publish the full plan for remigration?', 'Will you answer reports that MI5 were monitoring Dan Sambrook?', 'Would you describe the memo as racist, Mr Farage?'

Even GB News does a better job of breaking ground on the story than BBC News: it carries a report estimating that Sambrook is making £100,000 a month from a Substack founded after he was fired from Downing Street.

Tuesday, 8 January 2030, 9 a.m.

With the DG gone and the BBC in meltdown, Farage, ever the opportunist, spots his chance to close the licence fee discussions. He holds a press conference the next day to announce the outcome. 'Recent events have shown that the BBC cannot be trusted to spend public money in a way which reflects the full breadth of political views in this country. Time and time again it reverts to its narrow, metropolitan worldview that paints every Reform voter as racist. Therefore we are setting a requirement on the BBC to find 25 per cent worth of cuts this year and a further 20 per cent cuts in the year following, while retaining the programmes and services beloved by people up and down this country. We are pleased to have started well by saving licence fee payers the salary of the Corporation's useless former DG.'

A threat to the licence fee has previously brought the BBC's board to the verge of staging a mass resignation.

WHAT IF REFORM WINS

In 2010, one former board member was summoned to an emergency board meeting on the phone to discuss whether they should all resign because George Osborne was intending to dramatically reduce the BBC's income. A discussion ensued and one by one the members were asked to say whether they would back the plan. According to a person on the call, the chairman 'foolishly' asked someone who was fiercely against resigning to speak first and that emboldened others in their opinion. Once three people had said they wouldn't resign, there was no possibility of the board as a whole taking a stand and the plan collapsed. 'But it was a serious proposal by the chairman and he was very happy to resign himself,' the source said. In this scenario, following the press conference, the board chooses to use the single strongest weapon it has to register its objection. The chair, deputy chair and the entire board of the BBC, except from those who have been appointed by Whitehall or the devolved nations, announce their resignations with immediate effect – 'Find someone else to do your dirty work,' one board member tells Dan Jukes on the phone.

Wednesday, 9 January 2030, 9.45 a.m.

With the DG dispensed with over the 'Rivers of Blood' memo scandal and the chair, along with his board, out of the building in protest over the licence fee, Farage and Tice have free rein to appoint who they like to run the national broadcaster. They begin appointing a new chair, deputy chair and board members. The process has long been a chance for Labour and Tory governments to introduce one of their own at the top of the organisation: in 2001, for example, Labour-backer and friend of Prime Minister Gordon Brown, Gavyn Davies, was appointed chairman to a chorus of objections from the right-wing press. Given the unprecedented situation, Farage could go to the Privy Council and request that the King appoint a chair immediately. The monarch has little or no option but to agree to such a request from the prime minister.

In this scenario, Farage selects the 81-year-old Paul Dacre, former editor-in-chief of the *Daily Mail*, who has resigned as editor-in-chief of Associated Newspapers and from his Reform Party membership: 'I am committed to the role of the BBC in public life and to its mission of impartiality. There is a culture of left-wing bias in the BBC, as the recent strike by some BBC staff has shown, as well as comments by some of its biggest stars, and as chairman, I intend to lead a process of change and renewal at the broadcaster.'

Despite the plan in 2010, a situation in which the entire non-politically appointed board has resigned in protest is not covered in the Royal Charter. With Dacre established, he sets about bringing together an interim board to run the BBC while he makes the argument to the government that a new Charter is required to recognise the crisis the BBC is in. Dacre then sets about choosing a deputy and goes to the four nations who have a say in deciding one member of the board each – 'They could put five people in place pretty rapidly,' a former BBC executive said.

In a situation where nationalists are the largest party in Scotland and Sinn Fein are the biggest in Northern Ireland, it is likely they will choose politically aligned candidates. In this scenario, Reform are the largest party in Wales, but if it were Plaid Cymru, they would copy Northern Ireland and Scotland. From the start, the BBC board could be one which would be dominated by nationalist interests. Even if every member of the board did not resign and the appointed nations' representatives remained to run the BBC, such a situation is potentially 'more scary' for the broadcaster: in 2025, none of the members representing the nations had experience running a significant-sized board of a business and lack public confidence, having been appointed by politicians. With a board established, it falls to Dacre to begin the process of choosing a new DG.

Tuesday, 12 February 2030, 8 a.m.

The National Union of Journalists and the Bectu union stage a mass walkout, which cripples the majority of BBC services. The channels air endless repeats of *Fawlty Towers* and *Mrs Brown's Boys*, while on Radio 4 they broadcast an 'Archers Marathon' for 18 hours straight, interspersed with the shipping forecast and the weather. A 'budget version' of *Strictly* is also in the works. *The Times* carries a letter signed by the heads of a dozen press freedom charities, including Index and Reporters Without Borders, condemning 'government interference on an industrial level' in the BBC. *Race Across the World* is set in the UK for the first time to save on travel expenses. Benedict Cumberbatch and Martin Freeman agree to work on a new attempt at a series of *Sherlock* in a bid to make some money for the organisation. Later that day, the Council of Europe makes international headlines as it posts a sharp critique of the measures being passed by Parliament. The *New York Times* carries the story on its front page with the headline: '"Auntie" was once the world's most trusted news source. What happened?' Inside, the editorial opines that 'it is the darkest moment for the embattled news organisation, now led by a former tabloid journalist Tsar. A jewel in Britain's tarnished crown has been lost forever.'

A clip of George Osborne talking about the BBC on his podcast in 2024 is being shared on social media: 'I don't think government should have that kind of control over the BBC and I regret to some degree using that leverage. And I certainly regret, when I realise how much power the government had, not using the opportunity to put in some real protections for the BBC.'

That afternoon, a global poll by Gallup shows that the BBC has lost its position as the world's most trusted news brand. Farage, celebrating the passage of his legislation cancelling subsidies for renewables, takes a moment to give praise to an interviewer for the work of the new chair and promises the beginning of a 'new and truly impartial episode in the BBC's history'.

6

Up in Smoke

FOUR WEEKS BEFORE
REFORM'S SECOND BUDGET

Wednesday, 30 October 2030, 11.30 a.m.

The British Ambassador to the European Union requests an urgent meeting with Downing Street's foreign affairs private secretary. After their call, the official makes his way through No 10's warren of rooms, down a corridor and into the outer office adjoining the prime minister's study. He is initially refused entry: Farage is locked in crisis talks with Health Secretary Robert Jenrick about the staffing crisis in the NHS following the imposition of a stricter visa regime by the Home Office. But when he tells the PM's inner circle what he knows, one of them knocks on the door and asks if they can spare a moment.

The atmosphere inside the crowded room becomes ever more funereal as the private secretary speaks: 'I have very bad news, Prime Minister. I've heard from our man in Brussels that the Council will be issuing a statement tomorrow that in its view, Britain has violated the trade agreement by leaving the ECHR.'

The agreement the private secretary is referring to is the Trade and Cooperation Agreement (TCA), signed in December 2020 by Boris Johnson. Along with the Withdrawal Agreement, it governs Britain's entire post-Brexit relationship with the EU. The TCA is formed of three parts: a free trade agreement which sets rules on economic, social, environmental and fisheries issues; a framework for cooperation on security and criminal matters; and an overarching governance arrangement for resolving issues. It stipulates that either party can decide to leave it by giving one year's notice, or within just 30 days if either feels the other has committed a 'serious and substantial failure' to uphold 'essential elements' of the Agreement, for example on human rights. For Britain, leaving would mean the most significant economic upheaval imaginable: tariffs imposed on goods and services, customs checks causing chaos at the border, and a sea battle over fishing rights. European goods would vanish from supermarket shelves and house prices could take a knock due to the uncertainty. Four weeks before the Budget, Britain is facing a no-deal Brexit scenario and this time there is even less of a plan.

'According to our ambassador, the Netherlands prime minister was very persuasive and argued the British prime minister needed to be taught a lesson,' the official said. 'The Taoiseach begged them not to do it because of the impact on the Irish economy, but the rest of them overruled her. France blames us for causing migrant applications to spike over there, so they were easy to persuade.' There had been warnings from their ambassadors about the risks as the Great Repeal Bill was passing, but they hadn't taken them seriously. By firing a massive broadside at the moment of maximum fiscal jeopardy just before the Budget, the European Union are playing Reform at their own game.

'It's a threat, they'll never actually go through with it,' another advisor says. 'It's a negotiating tactic.'

'If they were going to do it, they'd have done it when the GRB passed. It's economic suicide.'

But the broadside has not come out of nowhere. Since Farage stood on the steps of Downing Street and announced he was immediately applying for Britain to rip up the ECHR, his whole premiership has been gripped by rising tensions with the EU. The bloc immediately suspended the TCA's law enforcement chapter in protest, as many had predicted. This had made policing, extradition and data-sharing with the EU almost impossible.

In response, Farage began making impossible demands for alterations to the Withdrawal Agreement, which governed amongst other things Northern Ireland's relationship with the EU and the status of Europeans in the UK. When the Democratic Unionist Party (DUP) refused to comply with a directive from the EU, despite them having an obligation to under Britain's post-Brexit deal, Farage took their side in exchange for their support in Parliament to pass legislation. There were disturbances on the streets of Belfast, which Brussels blamed on Farage's aggression and his disregard for the fragile peace in Northern Ireland.

'Mr Farage is acting recklessly with the great achievement of the Good Friday Agreement and peace in his country,' the German prime minister told reporters in the hallway of a summit in January. In protest at what he called 'foreign meddling in Britain's politics', Farage threatened to rip up the Withdrawal Agreement to bring the EU back to the negotiation table. Brussels observers had said doing so itself was a red line for the EU, so some were surprised when they did not immediately terminate the TCA then.

Negotiations had ensued and old wounds from the Brexit days were reopened, with talks ending in acrimony. On immigration, once they had left the ECHR, the Reform Cabinet believed they didn't need the help of their European neighbours: attempts to cross the Channel spiked in the first months after the election, but Farage's poll numbers climbed as he sent in the Navy and crossings declined.

On trade, as far back as the 2024 election manifesto, Reform had promised it wanted to 'prepare for negotiations over the TCA', with Farage vowing to 'stop EU fishers taking

UK quotas'. In this scenario, once he is in government, as one Reform watcher says, Farage takes the attitude that 'if the EU are pissed off, so be it'. During the spat following his threat on the Withdrawal Agreement, Farage uses meetings to demand Britain diverge aggressively on a whole host of regulations which he thinks are hampering growth, with his ire particularly reserved for a tariff on British steel which the bloc is threatening. He also takes issue with EU demands for the UK to pay billions of pounds into its defence fund, while charging countries like Canada less, and the hit British manufacturing was taking, in his view, from having to comply with the bloc's carbon border adjustment mechanism, which he blames for increasing inflation. By 2029, Britain under Labour had moved far closer to the EU in a whole host of areas as the former prime minister had made a dash for growth before the election. He calls Starmer's deal on youth mobility 'lunacy' and threatens to pull out of it entirely after an EU request for more leniency on visas – 'Labour have bound us to a failing economic bloc in such a way that it is very difficult to unpick,' Farage complains to *Bloomberg*.

Despite the friction, no one thought the Europeans would have the courage to press the nuclear button and terminate the TCA. But now, in the PM's office, it begins to dawn on his advisors that they had underestimated how much leaving the ECHR, with its implications for the precious peace in Northern Ireland, had enraged their former sparring partners in Brussels.

11.35 a.m.

Unaware of the situation developing next door, the chancellor is putting the finishing touches to his masterpiece. Richard Tice is walking the finest of economic lines: on one hand, Reform's tiny majority in the Commons means he must offer red meat in the form of tax cuts to his MPs, so the Budget passes and the government survives another day; and on the other, he must seem miserly enough with handouts so he can placate the markets and show he can service Britain's huge £2.7 trillion debt pile.

He also has to please the Office for Budget Responsibility (OBR), the powerful official forecaster who will mark Tice's homework immediately after his speech in the Commons. The OBR is important to chancellors because the markets will be watching its verdict closely, and Tice is desperate to avoid spooking investors. Under normal circumstances, there are three main steps making up the process the Treasury goes through before the publication of the OBR's forecast on the day of the Budget: first, the chancellor sets the date and gives 10 weeks' notice, while information is exchanged between it and officials; next, the Treasury gives the OBR a list of possible tax and welfare measures, and submits final 'major measures' three weeks before finally, last-minute minor updates are made on the latest data before the chancellor makes his or her speech. According to a person familiar with the process, there is little flexibility in the dates because they are already set up to make sure the process runs as quickly as possible, giving the chancellor very little room for manoeuvre if something knocks their work off course at the last minute. In this scenario, there are only days to go before Tice has to submit his policies to the OBR so they can generate a forecast, and give his work the all-important seal of approval. In 2022, Liz Truss's refusal to deal with the OBR in advance of her mini-budget was seen by the markets as reckless and this is a perception it is vital for Reform to avoid. Sat in his office in No 11, Tice doesn't know it yet but the delicate chess game of spending and prediction has been tossed in the air by the events happening next door.

This cautious fiscal strategy was a path set by his predecessor Robert Jenrick, and was something Farage ordered Tice to continue. During the election campaign, he had worked skilfully to make Reform's economic policy a genuinely national offering, speaking to former Labour mining towns as well as Tory shires. Like any chancellor, now he was in government it took a certain amount of dexterity to placate those different constituencies. At the same time, he also has to manage to retain unity within a party which had spent much of its existence before government as a protest movement, and lacks ideological coherence.

For example, whereas Tice is a traditional Thatcherite focused on energy and fiscal policy, as well as pensions, his colleague Zia Yusuf is from the new school of right-wing thinking, influenced by Silicon Valley and Farage's chief advisor, Cummings. Yusuf and Tice regularly lock horns in Cabinet and Yusuf's more radical approach has won fans among the business executives drafted in to sit around Farage at the long table in Downing Street. It didn't help that before he resigned, Cummings attended Cabinet meetings and sniped from the sidelines. But Reform insiders stress both men are 'very keen' on spending cuts across the board and agree with Farage that Britain needs fiscal consolidation before tax cuts.

'I've made it clear we cannot promise immediate tax cuts until we tackle the debt crisis created by the Conservatives and Labour,' Farage wrote in a 'Letter to the Nation' published in response to Rachel Reeves' Budget of 2025.

11.40 a.m.

A call from Jenrick, who is in the PM's office, lights up his phone. Tice ignores it: the last thing he needs is advice from a treacherous predecessor. He is busy reviewing the success of his measures from the previous year. A year ago, at his first Budget, Tice was widely considered to have struck the right balance. Left with a fiscal 'black hole' by Labour, who had spent big on cost of living measures before the election to try and see off the

Reform threat, he had opted for conservative measures popular among Reform voters. They had given tax breaks to family farms, cut subsidies to onshore wind farms and begun public sector pension reforms, his personal obsession. Buoyed by their success at the ballot box, MPs had remained unified enough to pass a Budget which cut benefits to foreign nationals, reduced foreign aid by £7 billion a year and hiked the immigration health surcharge from £1,035 to £2,718, which they claimed was the true cost of providing care to foreigners. Their cuts to disability allowances for those with anxiety and depression had allowed them to funnel over £3.5 billion to Border Force to begin setting up new processing facilities and removal units. Reform made a show of respecting the OBR, who had attacked their plans no more than they had Labour's, even though they hated how much power had been bestowed on them by the Liz Truss meltdown and then Starmer-era reforms in 2024. Instead of going after the OBR, Tice chose an easier target: the City watchdog. The Financial Conduct Authority (FCA), which oversees industry conduct and consumer protection, had been in Reform's sights for years after the quango had not backed Farage during the Coutts 'de-banking' scandal. The party leader had accused the FCA of a 'whitewash' after its report had found no evidence of people being refused services based on their political views. Tice resolved to clip its wings and transfer its powers back to the Bank of England in a move that was part of a broader strategy to cosy up to the City.

'They're pitching to the City for sure, massively,' one Reform-supporting think-tank staffer said. 'There's a fair bit of latent support for their agenda and they want to find it. They all hate the FCA. They despise the FCA, it's such a terrible regulator.' Reform's deregulation agenda had seen funds from the financial sector flow into the Party's war chest before the election and Tice was keen to keep them happy ahead of the May 2031 local elections. It wasn't exciting, but it had worked: the Party, the City and the bond markets were on side.

11.43 a.m.

A text from Yusuf flashes up on Tice's phone: 'Get in the den now'. Tice is used to being bullied by those around Farage – he sees no need to rush next door. As he ambles through the warren of corridors separating Nos 10 and 11, he feels confident that this year he can go further. Now they have shown the markets they can be trusted to make difficult decisions on the economy and deliver reductions in spending, they can begin fulfilling their fiscal ambitions. Reform backbenchers are salivating for tax cuts and there are anonymous reports in the newspapers about growing dissent in the parliamentary tearoom at Tice's lack of courage.

In their 2024 'Contract', the Party had vowed to raise the threshold when people started to pay income tax from £12,570 to £20,000 to encourage those on low incomes into work and off benefits. In his response to Rachel Reeves' Budget of 2025, Farage repeated his desire to raise thresholds 'as soon as possible'. While the language had become more limited in the years following the 2024 election, lifting millions of people out of income tax is the Party's greatest fiscal aspiration. But when Tice had threatened to enact the policy in front of Treasury officials, they had pleaded with him to see sense and recognise it was far too expensive.

'Chancellor, our best estimates show it would cost more than £41 billion. It would spook the markets and the Budget would fall apart,' the permanent secretary had warned the year previously.

But after the success of his first budget, and with more spending reductions planned, Tice had obtained backing from Farage to begin the process. Tice's media SpAd set about placing a series of leaks to get voters, and Reform MPs, excited. A string of stories reported the chancellor was going to raise the threshold from £12,570 to £15,000.

His 'rabbit in the hat' was that he was going to raise the threshold by an extra £2,000 to £17,000 at a cost to the Exchequer of tens of billions of pounds. He had already sent off sections of the Budget containing his tax plans to the OBR and had privately received encouraging noises that if he got government spending down to the right place, they would rubber-stamp the tax cut.

11.48 a.m.

Tice arrives in the Cabinet Room – a place that witnessed Winston Churchill declaring Victory in Europe and Clement Attlee founding the NHS – and before he even knocks on the door of Farage's adjoining study, he can hear the pandemonium inside. As a shaken official explains the news from Brussels, the chancellor looks as though he's going to throw up. Zia Yusuf is complaining about the Wi-Fi as Jenrick stands in the corner, scribbling something unintelligible on a whiteboard. Farage's head is in his hands as he listens to an economic advisor outlining the ramifications of the EU's statement: there would be a lethal hit to the economy from going on to World Trade Organization (WTO) terms and they should immediately start reheating no-deal Brexit scenarios, known as 'Operation Yellowhammer', to prepare the country.

More than six months of painstaking work on the Budget is at risk, with only a week before Tice has to deliver his final plans for the OBR.

Tice begs Farage to go back to the EU and attempt a negotiation: 'We are Europe's third-largest trading partner. This is going to tank their economy too. It's in literally nobody's interests.'

'It's in our interests, actually,' Dan Jukes says, still riding high after his victory over the BBC. 'This is the battle we've been looking for. Some boring Eurocrat comes out of nowhere and tanks our economy because of "human rights". He's the perfect villain. Fuck him!'

'This is ridiculous. Don't you see? Don't you realise what cuts we're going to have to make to make this budget work?'

'Surely there's more that can go? Why do you need so many hangers on for a start?' Farage says, gesturing to Tice's entourage, who have trailed in behind him.

Tice gets up and slams the door on his way out.

1.30 p.m.

Dan Jukes leaks the story to the *Telegraph* that the EU are about to rip up their post-Brexit trading agreement. *Best to get ahead of it*, he thought, *and control the framing.* Across the front pages, the press fall on predictable lines: the *Telegraph* and the *Mail* pick up on his 'stab in the back' line, while the *Guardian* cast it as a correct retort to Reform taking a wrecking ball to human rights.

That evening, he rides home in a black cab past Steve Bray, the Stop Brexit campaigner, who has reappeared again outside Downing Street. Like back in 2016, Britain once again was about to tear itself apart over its relationship with Europe.

Overnight, the pound falls sharply against the dollar and yen, and FTSE futures also drops on Asian markets. When the City wakes the next morning, it is going to be choppy.

Thursday, 31 October 2030, 6 a.m.

The statement from the European Union drops on *Politico*'s website early the next morning. Its wording is pored over by Westminster, Fleet Street and the City: the EU threatens the termination of the TCA 'if' Britain does not 'see sense under its obligations'.

The statement cites the EU's right to take this course of action if there has been a 'serious and substantial failure' to uphold the 'essential elements' of the agreement.

UK equities plummet by 5 per cent, with the British-dominated FTSE 250 hit particularly hard. On the credit markets, spreads widen, especially on industries with the most EU exposure, such as car manufacturing and logistics. Unsurprisingly the market takes the view that the news creates a higher recession risk in the UK, and that the Bank of England would have to cut interest rates sooner. This leads bond investors to buy up more short-term gilts, meaning their yield drops quickly. A graph on the FT's homepage shows the steepening yield curve. An official in No 10 tells Tice in an urgent meeting what all this means for the cost of Britain's £2.5 trillion debt obligation: 'The cost of issuing gilts is rapidly increasing due to the uncertainty as investors take fright at what the state of the UK economy will be like long term without the TCA. At the moment, about 70 per cent of gilts are long-term, so if those yields rise by just 0.3 basis points, we are going to be paying more than £5 billion more in interest payments. That figure has just passed 0.25 and is rising.' The City traders who control the bond markets were as close as they had ever been to pulling the plug on the Reform government. Everything now depended on the reaction to the budget.

Farage sends Yusuf out on to the airwaves in an attempt to calm things down. 'Well, is that surprising?' he tells the BBC's *Today* programme. 'It's more sabre rattling from the Eurocrats. This is a toothless threat, they're terrified our demands on trade will sink their feeble economy. Europe is a failed state and the quicker someone kicks in the door and the rotten house crumbles, the better.' Unsurprisingly, this is felt to be far from reassuring and the yield curve continues to climb.

In a separate statement to *Politico*, Mr Sågfors, the EU's chief negotiator, points out the 'essential elements' Britain agreed to when it signed the TCA were commitments to 'democracy' and the 'rule of law and human rights'.

'It is sad to see the country of *habeas corpus* and the Magna Carta leave the ECHR to become a rogue state alongside Russia and Belarus,' he says, but when *Today*'s presenter Anna Foster pushes him on when the bloc will formally submit the termination, Sågfors evades the answer. Despite European countries' distress at Britain's vandalism of their agreement, and their deep frustration at the war of words with Farage since he became PM, he knows a 'no deal' scenario will be a crippling hit for dozens of Europe's most important industries.

Farage goes on to TikTok to lambast the EU for their 'stab in the back': 'Listening to the EU chief negotiator this morning, I don't think I have ever in my life witnessed such an unspeakably dishonourable act of vandalism and treachery. I have spent my life battling with these men in Brussels and they never learn, do they? They never learn that this country will not – and cannot – be bullied.'

That night, a snap poll by YouGov shows the public back the prime minister, with 55 per cent of people seeing the EU's criticism of the UK leaving the ECHR as an unacceptable overreach into a country which had opted out of its community 13 years previously. On seeing the polling, Farage is delighted: he loves nothing more than a fight with his old enemies across the Channel.

2.30 p.m.

Although the Bank of England is officially independent, Tice spends his day on the phone to the Labour-appointed governor. The Bank has a responsibility to intervene to help markets to function and keep inflation low. The chancellor's principal private secretary spends all day in talks with the governor's private secretary to work out a plan, and eventually the governor decides to intervene to buy sterling to stabilise the fluctuating conditions. An *FT* analysis states that 'today, Britain has come the closest to a Liz Truss-style meltdown that we've seen in five years. If Mr Sågfors had put his money where his mouth was today and actually submitted the termination of the TCA, the UK economy would have tipped over the edge. With the Budget just days away, and the OBR beginning to assess the Chancellor's plans, the EU has just piled pressure on to this fledgling Reform government.'

8 p.m.

The chancellor calls his permanent secretary, who maps out how the Treasury will respond to the crisis. It is fortunate the department – the most powerful in Whitehall – has mostly protected itself from cuts. He informs Tice he has already called the OBR, who advise him that they have secretly been working on a separate forecast looking at the economic impact of the EU terminating the TCA, given the rising political tension. However, they would still need the new budget measures by the deadline if the OBR were to revise the figures.

There is precedence for flexibility during the forecast preparation process: for example, when Russia invaded Ukraine in February 2022, the effect on global markets led to revisions in the month leading up to Rishi Sunak's Spring Statement.[25] But a catastrophe of the size of a

---

[25] The other example is the budget of March 2020, where the OBR's forecast was out of date by the time it was published as Whitehall scrambled to put in place coronavirus measures. In that instance, there was no time to change their predictions. But in this scenario, with four weeks before the budget, investors would expect Tice to make the numbers add up.

no-deal trading arrangement with the EU is almost unprecedented and the Treasury has precious little time to balance the books.

Next, the permanent secretary orders a late-night video call with his executive committee, known as EXCO, comprised of the Treasury's four or five director generals (DGs), including the chief economist. At least two of them think saving the Budget is impossible and advise their boss to tell Tice as much. One of them is close to tears as the discussion turns to the eye-watering cuts they will have to make to public services, most of which will fall on the most vulnerable. The permanent secretary knows that if he raises objections to the chancellor, he will destroy his carefully calibrated relationship with the new regime and he will be fired. The last time a permanent secretary was shown the door, when Sir Tom Scholar was let go by Kwasi Kwarteng in 2022 at the height of the Liz Truss meltdown, it was considered a key reason for spooking the markets.

'It's out of the question,' he tells them, before asking them to begin standing up a team. In the Treasury, there's a division called Strategy, Planning and Budget (SPB): 'They're your fixers,' according to one former official. The SPB will immediately set about assembling a 'surge team' of their finest officials to work on saving the Budget – 'They will pluck people out of their jobs, people who can hack the hours and who are high performers.' The officials will work all hours to analyse what spending cuts have been identified so far by Tice and forecast what would happen if they went further.

The surge team will work closely with a team who, in the words of a former employee, 'really run the government'. This unit rejoices in the intriguingly nondescript name of General Expenditure Policy (GEP) and are the custodians of the list detailing all the major line items of government spend, otherwise known as the 'Stack'. The Stack is what is haggled over during spending reviews, when the Treasury has to fend off 'asks' from Whitehall departments. The surge team and the GEP will pore over the Stack to strip out billions of pounds of savings, and officials and Treasury SpAds will begin negotiations with their counterparts across government. Under Reform, with so many new ministers and special advisors, there are still dozens of advisors across Whitehall who the Treasury team barely know, slowing the process down. This time, the process is less negotiation and more diktat, as Tice's powerful advisors work through department by department and policy area by policy area to force excruciating efficiencies on ministers. Two threaten to resign on the spot, one wipes away tears with his turquoise tie and another vows to cause chaos by green-lighting a series of insane policy decisions, something which had become known internally as 'doing a Lee Anderson' in reference to the former home secretary's handling of migrant hotels.

The Treasury building on 1 Horse Guards is very different from the labyrinthine Downing Street: it's open-plan and the permanent secretary sits in the middle alongside the troops. For the next few days, there's a buzz like an old Fleet Street newsroom before the print deadline as minister after minister barrels into Tice's office, only to exit some 20 minutes later, attempting to look insouciant. Their entourage of advisors do a less good job as they nervously tap into their phones as they head for the lift.

But the atmosphere on the department floor only tells half the story: the Treasury has ordered hundreds of officials from around Whitehall to aide it and there's not enough space for them all. Under 1 Horse Guards, the Treasury has access to a basement which connects to the Cabinet War Rooms, built in 1938 because of the threat of German bombing. The permanent secretary directs the most important members of the surge unit and the GEP to position themselves underground in the wartime shelters, away from the comings and goings of ministers.

WHAT IF REFORM WINS

Wednesday, 27 November 2030, 9 a.m.

Budget Day. It's Treasury tradition that officials involved in putting together the measures enjoy a 'Budget breakfast' and are given a free voucher for the canteen. In true Treasury style, there's a strict list of who worked on it: there are no freeloaders. Officials mutter into their baked beans as they await Tice's hour of judgement.

11.30 a.m.

Tice appears with the red box outside No 11, giving his best matinée-idol smile for the cameras. On Downing Street, the BBC's Faisal Islam tells viewers that 'the chancellor has only himself to blame. After dangling the possibility of raising the lowest rate of tax, he's painted himself into a corner and he's now predicted to have to make deep cuts to public services so the sums add up. It has been one of the most chaotic run-ups to a chancellor's speech in a long time, including the farce in 2025 when Rachel Reeves' plans were leaked by the OBR half an hour before she took to the dispatch box. The markets are extremely jittery over fresh drama with the EU and will be watching very carefully to see if Tice has the political capacity to actually drive through the spending cuts he is promising.' No chancellor in living memory has allowed so much to ride on a single speech.

12.30 p.m.

The chancellor stands and takes a sip of single malt whisky. Tradition dictates this is the only occasion when alcohol is permitted in the chamber of the House of Commons. Just over a month ago, Tice had trailed to the *Express* that he was excited to be the 'first Chancellor since Kenneth Clarke in 1996 to claim his right to have a tipple during his speech'.

The team around Farage had loved the idea. 'The year after was when it all went wrong for Britain,' one of his aides said, thinking of the 1997 election and the horrors of Blair and Brown. 'It will be a sign things are back to normal.'

Tice's sip from a crystal glass feels ridiculous now: the government benches are eerily quiet. MPs shift in their seats, unsure of how the OBR would deem the chancellor's measures after the desperate last-minute rush. Rather than a defiant return to the traditions of the Commons, parliamentary sketchwriters start drafting their intros about a chancellor drunk at the steering wheel of the nation's finances.

The chancellor begins by attacking the legacy left by Labour: 'A front bench who allowed their fiscal policy to be controlled by their socialist backbenchers, entrenched welfare dependency for those of working age, a hatred of business and anyone trying to make a profit in this country.' He then moves into the simple stuff he knows will gee-up his MPs: a reduction in Whitehall headcount by 30 per cent and severe cuts to disability spending in schools for 'overdiagnosed' conditions; attacking the Opposition for spending £52 million on a 'road to nowhere' in Guyana, £100 million on family planning initiatives in Pakistan and billions on heat pumps that are a 'load of dysfunctional hot air'.

There are some encouraging grunts from his backbenches, but not half as much as usual. Fewer are wearing turquoise ties than usual, he notices, as he swings around to address the Speaker. Everyone is waiting for the tax threshold announcement. Is he going to risk it?

'I am delighted to announce that a Reform government will once again make work pay. The current threshold stands at £12,570. We believe that is far too low. We will raise income tax thresholds not to £15,000, not to £16,000, but to £17,000 for the British worker. No more will it profit to sit on benefits, no more will Whitehall raid the pay packets of the public to pay for their wasteful spending, no more will those on the lowest incomes be penalised by the State.'

The bank of Reform MPs stands and cheers and applauds the measure. One Reform MP, wearing a top hat, opens his jacket to reveal a T-shirt emblazoned with the words: 'TAX CUTS FOR GREAT YARMOUTH NOW'. He pumps his fist to the camera. There is widespread ecstasy as MPs throw their order papers into the air, embrace, and stand on the green benches. A group of four members have somehow managed to smuggle in a huge Union flag in Reform colours, which they unfurl and raise aloft. They look like Delacroix's *Liberty Leading the People*, or the home terraces after a 90th-minute goal. It is a stunning victory whatever the costs, they think: their party has delivered one of the largest tax cuts in British history.

The Farage-friendly Speaker rises in his chair and barks furiously at the Opposition, who have risen to their feet in objection, to obey parliamentary decorum and sit. Once Reform MPs calm down, the chancellor maps out the 'judicious' cuts needed to pay for the 'uncertainty caused by the actions of Mr Sågfors and his friends' militant hatred of these islands'.

The list of reductions and economies is brutal. Tice sets a Spending Rule which mandates a reduction of 15 per cent per year on outgoings across all unprotected departments. In Water and Food Security new environmental farming schemes would be scrapped and the regulators will be cut back even further. He pauses spending on the 'disastrous' HS2, even though it is mostly finished, and praises the prime minister for ordering a review into the high-speed rail link. There was a prospect that Britain would be left with huge parts of railway infrastructure built, but with not enough money to actually to use it.

In the Department for Digital, Culture, Media & Sport (DCMS), museums and galleries will shutter as arts funding is all but abolished, and local sports teams will cease to practice as sports grants dry up. Debt interest payments were one of the few areas given protection. Some post-16 education will become fee-paying, Tice warns, and university fees will go up again. Charges for libraries and prescriptions will be hiked.

But Tice is not finished yet. He announces the abolition of the triple lock, which is costing the Treasury £15.5 billion a year in 2030, three times more than predicted. 'The actions of the Eurocrats in the last few weeks have brought Britain to the brink, but we are at our best when we have our backs against the wall,' Tice says.

Finally, he reveals that NHS services will be charged for at the point of use for the first time. It is a historic moment: the end of Aneurin Bevan's dream of universal healthcare after just over 80 years.

There is silence from the government benches, but the Opposition go berserk, and the shadow chancellor lambasts Tice as the 'enemy of the old, the sick, the young, families, and workers'.

Sitting towards the back, a group of Reform MPs is listening quietly. They are far from economic experts, but they know one thing: with Britain's trading relationship with the EU in peril, the bond markets are extremely volatile and the last thing the country's finances need is an unnecessary tax cut to the tune of tens of billions of pounds. When they go home to their constituencies at the end of the week, how will they explain why the hospital has to close, why their pension is worth less than it was last month and why the police can't seem to solve a crime? Their constituents believed that immigration had ruined Britain and it was Reform's mission to end it, but they were also telling them time and time again that the cost of living was just as important an issue to Britain as the small boats. Would the boost from the tax cut in people's accounts paper over the cracks? They were far from certain. The cabal, many of whom are former military veterans serving former Conservative seats, are relieved at only one thing: that, at a time of war in Europe, defence seems to have been protected. The Army is already on its knees and the safety of the realm is the first duty of government. As Tice's speech comes to an end, they resolve to meet up in the pub later to discuss what to do.

1 p.m.

The director of the Institute for Fiscal Studies (IFS) appears on BBC Radio 4's *World at One* to give his snap verdict.

'Before they came into government, Reform at least tried to talk seriously about running the nation's finances. They made an attempt to appear prudent in their first budget last year, but the mask today has slipped. Instead of removing his reckless tax cuts from his budget, Tice and Farage – and we must remember who really wears the trousers here – have chosen party unity over financial sense. Yes, I'm sure the cuts are achievable in theory, but with public services already cut to the bone, markets may take the view that these announcements are never actually going to come to fruition. But with a small majority, it only takes 20 or so Reform MPs to see sense and bring Downing Street to heel.'

1.30 p.m.

The OBR releases its study of the Budget proposals. The forecaster says the economy is in a 'vulnerable' state following Tice's new fiscal policies. 'The chance for the damaging global events to blow the British economy off course remains acute after this Budget. The full effects of the

EU's announcement on the TCA [Trade and Cooperation Agreement] have yet to be fully assessed, but the measures pile further pressure on the need for the chancellor to achieve extraordinary cuts to services, the likes of which Britain has not seen since the middle of the last century.'

In an interview afterwards, the head of the OBR mentions that he was surprised the chancellor did not tell the Commons about the cut to Trident, the UK's nuclear programme, in his Budget speech. The interviewer's eyes widen: very few in SW1 had noticed that buried in the small print of the published budget document, which policy specialists and market analysts scour as soon as it is released on gov.uk, Tice had ordered a reduction in Britain's nuclear deterrent, amounting to a huge cut in the defence budget. The interviewer knew it would go down extremely badly with some Reform MPs.

An hour later, Tice releases a statement: 'I'm taking tough decisions to deal with the shock caused by the stab in the back from the Eurocrats across the Channel. I can still cut taxes because I'm cutting spending to balance the books. I am content today that the OBR has said they are balanced. But there are few areas of government which can be left untouched due to the scale of the savings we have to make because of the uncertainty caused by the voiding of the Trade and Cooperation Agreement. I am today making the difficult decision to scale back our Trident nuclear defence capability to ease the burden of our efficiencies elsewhere.'

7 p.m.

The other Treasury tradition on Budget Day is for those who have toiled on the Budget – ministers, advisors and officials alike – to head to the Two Chairmen pub just around the corner from the *Spectator*'s offices on Dartmouth

Street following the chancellor's speech in the Commons. Even Rachel Reeves and her Treasury ministers made an unlikely appearance after the Spending Review, in 2025, with dozens of officials spilling across the road opposite the offices of *Prospect* Magazine and the Resolution Foundation. This year, there are even more than usual, given the dramatic circumstances leading up to the day.

There is plenty of gossip among the assembled about how the radical cuts to tax and spending would go down with Reform MPs. A vote on the Budget is different from other deliberations in the Commons: it is seen as a vote of confidence in the administration itself. It is true that if the government loses a vote on a specific measure in the Budget, as it did when Ken Clarke was Chancellor in 1994 over an increase in VAT on fuel, it can come back to the House with new proposals on how it will find the extra revenue, but if the government lost a vote on a key plank of the bill, it will affect its ability to raise revenue and therefore to govern.

There are two stages in the process by which the Commons passes a Budget: the first is a series of votes and debates giving provisional support to the measures, and then a vote on a Finance Bill formalises them. The debates usually take place over four days and divisions will occur on significant or controversial elements during that period. One 'resolution' must be passed so a Finance Bill can begin to be put together, and this is where the jeopardy lies for Tice: if he loses that vote, the Budget collapses.

Tice feels confident enough to show his face at the Two Chairmen. Proud to have taken a few pennies off the cost of alcohol duty, he poses with a pint of Madri for a TikTok video filmed by one of his aides. There is a mood of general excitement among the politicians present about the income tax cut and many MPs keen to ingratiate themselves with the chancellor approach him to kiss the ring and take a selfie. The meaning and scale of the cuts has not sunk in.

It is as if when they had heard about the giveaway, everything else was a footnote. They had been chosen for loyalty, after all, not the ability to scrutinise legislation. Inside the pub, however, tucked away in a dark corner, sit five sombre-looking Reform MPs. None of the journalists know who they are; they are left alone to talk. They are in the process of forming a Reform Veterans Group, having decided to pool their expertise, given that all have campaigned against cuts to military spending by successive governments.

Thursday, 28 November 2030, 9.30 a.m.

After the excitement of the day before subsides, Reform MPs are experiencing a sharp hangover. Their email inboxes are flooded with letters from outraged constituents terrified at the effect the cuts will have on them when their finances are already so strained. *The Times* reports that a faction of Reform MPs crowded into the chief whips' office to call for the prime minister to listen to their demands late last night.

The front page of the *Telegraph* reads: 'Tice takes a chainsaw to the triple lock.'

12 p.m.

As if from nowhere, like mushrooms on the forest floor, white tents begin to appear on the lawn of College Green. The advisors in the Policy Unit watch the spores spread throughout the afternoon as the world's media start to sniff drama. The number of MPs posting their dissent for the Budget grows from two to three, to seven, to nine. GB News even installs a 'ticking time bomb' with Farage's face on it at the bottom of their screen, counting the number of MPs who have publicly stated their displeasure. The majority of Reform MPs are still loyal, but there are dozens who are hiding their anger: MPs who have felt shut out of government, like a substitute never called on to the pitch; MPs who thought they'd get a chance to run something or make a difference, only to be bullied by whips and passed over for ministerial positions; MPs who felt embarrassed to be part of a government which had climbed down over the Falklands and turned Bristol into a swamp. Those who thought their immigration policy had gone too far, those who thought they had been a soft touch and wanted to send all illegal migrants to the Ascension Islands. Those who missed *Antiques Roadshow*, *Countryfile*, and *The Repair Shop*, all of which the BBC had cancelled to save money, and those who actually thought in some instances heat pumps were quite impressive bits of kit.

For a moment that afternoon, the markets begin to strengthen and Tice thinks that the storm may have blown over. This lasts mere minutes as one official points out that traders are coming to the view that Tice is finished, and that the prospect of a less shambolic Budget is becoming possible.

12.10 p.m.

A shaky live stream of a French reporter rushing up to Mr Sågfors outside a bistro in Brussels appears on the BBC.

Speaking in French, the journalist asks: 'Monsieur, what do you make of the chaos the EU decision to revoke the TCA is causing in the UK? Mr Farage has accused member states of a "treacherous act of sabotage". How do you respond?'

Mr Sågfors says, 'Excuse me, I have to attend a lunch. The Budget is a domestic affair on which I will not comment, but I will say this: if you do not want to be a part of Europe or the Convention, then you cannot expect the Treaty, which was interwoven by Boris Johnson and the EU into our agreements, to remain the same. Many very good British lawyers have warned for many years that the Agreement could be terminated at any time if politicians recklessly exit the ECHR. Now you will have a British Bill of Rights. But it seems Mr Farage has decided the British will not only have limited human rights, but they should also be poor.'

Mr Sågfors' eyes sparkle with something close to mirth behind his round tortoiseshell spectacles as he turns and pushes through the bistro's curtained entranceway.

12.15 p.m.

Farage is furiously berating his whips' office to do something, anything, they can to prevent a collapse in support for the measures. His strategy is to pick off the five leading MPs behind the sudden flurry of dissent one by one: he offers the Minister for Veterans job to one, he threatens another with screenshots of Facebook posts made in support of the BNP 20 years ago, he promises backing of a new hospital in another. His party has been loyal so far but beneath the appearance of acquiescence, there has been a growing sense that Downing Street is taking them for granted; that Dan Jukes, Zia Yusuf and Arron Banks got to swagger around SW1 while the Reform foot soldiers who kept them in power were mere 'lobby fodder' to pass legislation.

Even now, with the government teetering on the brink, Reform MPs on the Thatcherite wing of the Party stand in resolution debates to praise the chancellor for lifting millions out of tax. But for the 'Blue Labour' side, who are keen to protect the role of the state in health and welfare, cutting public services to the bone to satisfy the bean counters at the OBR is not only wrong, but reckless when it comes to the lives of the public. When they were in opposition, hadn't Reform criticised the OBR and its undue influence on British politics?

As more and more get wind of the goodies being dealt out in exchange for shutting up, increasing numbers of MPs feel able to share their concerns. The whip's strategy is beginning to unravel fast.

3 p.m.

Opposition MPs see their chance and apply to the Speaker to table a motion of no confidence in the government as the tracker of dissenting Reform MPs shows 20. There are chaotic scenes in the division lobby as Reform whips, together with Chief Secretary to the Treasury Nadhim Zahawi, square up to one of the cabal of rebellious MPs who are set on voting against the government. One of the whips throws a punch at the former soldier, who grabs him by the lanyard and throws him to the floor. Three other MPs are filming the tussle as a pair of Labour MPs hold the whip back. The vote is abandoned as the Speaker swoops down from her seat and members of security arrive in the lobbies.

Farage is hiding in the prime minister's Commons office and chain-smoking furiously just metres away from the chaos. The door rattles as MPs of all colours jostle in the packed lobby: many of them haven't heard the vote has been cancelled and are shouting at the clerks, demanding to know why they are being kettled. In the scrum are Farage's chief whip and his deputy, who collar Arron Banks. Banks is one of the prime minister's oldest associates, one of the very few men who can give him hard news. The chief whip tells Banks that Farage's aides are whispering in the leader's ear that he can hang on.

Banks accepts his mission and manages to escape the crowd and prise open the door to see the prime minister. He informs Farage that the whipping operation to get the Budget through the Commons has failed, there are rumours that the group of MPs intending to vote against the government has grown to approximately 30 and while the vote has been delayed and the Speaker has adjourned the sitting, he may want to consider his position in order to save himself the final embarrassment. The sound of the prime minister screaming at Banks is only drowned out by the din in the voting lobbies. Farage will not listen to any of his MPs, who he believes would not be there without him and who are blind to the fact that, despite the Budget meltdown, the opinion polls are still in his favour. Donations are flooding in from supporters around the country, disgusted by the attacks on a leader they consider the most courageous since Thatcher, and from those comfortable enough to not be affected by many of the cuts.

'There is only one person I can think of who he'll listen to now,' Banks tells his aides.

5 p.m.

After security investigates the fight and an MP with a black eye is seen by the Commons' nurse, the vote of no confidence goes ahead. Farage narrowly loses by less than expected: in the end, 28 Reform MPs voted against their leader. Afterwards, the prime minister's motorcade is waiting in Old Palace Yard to whisk Farage away. It drives around Parliament Square, passing Robert Jenrick who is giving an interview praising Farage as a 'political trailblazer' but questioning whether there may be 'others who are better fitted to take Reform into the 2030s'. The driver tells Farage he 'should never have let in those Tories', but Farage says nothing. The car pulls into Horse Guards Parade, from where the PM returns to Downing Street. He takes the lift to his private flat above No 11 and when he opens the heavy Georgian door, he is surprised to see his wife, Laure, on the settee, sat waiting for him.

Laure doesn't tell him that she, like everyone else in the country, has been watching events on the news unfold all day and was just off the phone to Banks. Zia Yusuf has already posted his letter of resignation on X. He said he was 'disgusted' at the scale of the cuts and was resigning on a 'point of principle'. Suella Braverman follows suit moments later. The partner of a prime minister often ranks as the most important advisor in their court; a witness to the leader in their most vulnerable moments and their sole counsellor at the end of the day. Clementine Churchill warned her husband to check his 'rough sarcastic and overbearing manner' on becoming leader of the wartime coalition; Philip May listened to his wife Theresa as she resolved to call a general election in 2017; Denis Thatcher told his wife just before her resignation in 1990: 'You've done enough, old girl. For God's sake, don't go on any longer.'

Laure takes her husband's hand and explains that it is time to stop now. Although he blames Tice for the chaos in the Commons and says that fewer than expected voted against him, Farage realises the only way to get out of this mess is to suddenly resign. His Budget is in tatters, the market response will lead to a household bills shock, his agenda has been shredded by his desperate attempt to make the numbers add up. There seems to be no other way which preserves at least some of his dignity. In this scenario, Farage listens to his wife, then informs his closest aides of his decision. They beg him not to go, to roll the dice one last time. But he has realised the game is up, and stands on the steps of Downing Street and informs a relieved country of his decision. Tice, indelibly tainted by the budget fiasco, goes soon after. The aged King invites Robert Jenrick to become Prime Minister, but as he cannot reliably command the authority of the House, within weeks he asks the King to dissolve Parliament, with a fresh general election held in the hope a government will be returned with a working majority and a plan to clean up the mess.

7

Limpet

When asked to imagine Farage listening to someone telling him to stand down, one former Reform insider said: 'Nobody could do it, Nigel's an autocrat.' So, what would happen in this scenario if Farage doesn't listen to Laure, and decides he will not resign and will instead do everything in his power to remain in Downing Street?

What happens if a prime minister goes rogue?

Britain has, strangely, been in a situation where there has been uncertainty over whether a prime minister will 'do the decent thing' and resign within recent memory. In 2022, as dozens of ministers left Boris Johnson's government following the Pincher affair, for a queasy couple of days it was far from obvious whether Johnson – a leader who had already driven a coach and horses through Britain's constitutional arrangements – would resign. When the chairman of the 1922 Committee, which represents Conservative backbenchers, went to tell him the game was up, Johnson was reported to have told Sir Graham Brady: 'I don't believe you and even if it's true, then I'm going to fight. You can't force me out without an election. I'm going to fight to stay here.' The Reform Party constitution states that in order to trigger a leadership contest, at least 50 of the Party's MPs must vote against Farage.

In 2022, over the following day, briefings were made to the press that Johnson would not be resigning and was instead going to attempt to rebuild his government. The public were told there would be fresh ministerial appointments, but none came and it was only when his chancellor of two days – Nadhim Zahawi – wrote on X that Johnson had to go that he eventually informed the country as to his intentions.

The embarrassing demise of Johnson's government tested the 'good chaps' theory of government to its very limits. Popularised by Lord Peter Hennessy around 30 years ago, it describes how leaders, ministers and civil servants recognise the unspoken assumptions underpinning Britain's unwritten and informal constitution and act accordingly, and will resign if necessary. Unlike nearly every other democracy in the world, Britain does not have a set of rules outlining core principles or the role of institutions and procedures. This makes Britain unusually vulnerable to a politician using their political power beyond accepted norms by exploiting the informality of the country's traditional arrangements. Protections have been further degraded by the state of the House of Lords, which in a time of crisis lacks democratic legitimacy to check the Commons as it is not directly accountable to voters and has been filled with questionable appointments by a succession of prime ministers.

In this scenario, with a radical right-wing Reform government unable to pass a budget and teetering on the brink of collapse, and Farage as Prime Minister holed up in Downing Street, it is perfectly possible that he simply refuses to leave office. Even after a vote of no confidence in the Commons, Farage would be telling himself and those around him that he is ahead in the polls and this is an establishment stitch-up. In a phrase coined by Professor Andrew Blick and Hennessy, Downing Street will become a rockpool home to a 'limpet' prime minister.

LIMPET

Monday, 2 December 2030, 6 p.m.

When Farage loses the vote of no confidence in the Commons, a message from the King's private secretary Sir Clive Alderton lands in the inbox of the PM's principal private secretary, requesting an audience with Farage. He is saved in the PPS's contacts as 'Chris HMTK', the abbreviation used in government to refer to His Majesty The King. Close relationships between the three corners of the 'golden triangle' of the cabinet secretary, the prime minister's principal private secretary and the monarch's private secretary will be vitally important if the country is to survive the constitutional test presented by a 'limpet' prime minister and they will be in constant communication. But in this scenario, the constitutional power and influence of the first two have been degraded by the politicisation of their roles. While in previous governments these relations would have usually been smooth, under Farage's reforms the role of the cabinet secretary is now Chief Executive to the Prime Minister and the principal private secretary might have the same title but they are just as politicised.

With ministers resigning in protest and the prime minister intending to work into the night to appoint a new chancellor and Cabinet members, Farage has more important things to do than to be lectured by the monarch. The relationship with HMTK over his short stint in Downing Street has been very different to that under Keir Starmer: government sources in 2025 said there was a 'lot of respect' between the Palace and Downing Street and considerations to do with the King come up a 'surprising amount'. When writing a King's Speech, lots of care is taken by senior people in Downing Street over what is felt 'appropriate' for Charles to say.

Despite the mutual dislike, in practice Farage has little choice but to accept the King's demand, although he is confused as he knows the King is in poor health. Their weekly audiences have been sporadic in the last months. But as the nation saw in 2022 when Queen Elizabeth II summoned the strength to dismiss Boris Johnson and invite Liz Truss to form a government, the head of state will do everything in their power, even in ill health, to exercise their constitutional function. The King has the power to ask for a prime minister's resignation, but the use of such a power by a constitutional monarch in a scenario where a leader still enjoys considerable support in the country would make him vulnerable to the charge that he is conducting a coup against British democracy. As previously noted, the King does have the power to 'encourage', 'advise' and 'warn' a prime minister in an audience.

That night, Farage slips out of Downing Street without his motorcade and heads to the Palace. Charles struggles to stand when the PM enters and now walks with a cane. The King pleads with his prime minister to see sense, 'be a good chap' and resign.

But Farage insists he has the right to try again to retain the command the Commons and demands a day to exercise it.

Tuesday, 3 December 2030, 5 p.m.

George Cottrell, the prime minister's best fixer and one of his most loyal attendants, is a gambler. A minor aristocrat, Cottrell made headlines in 2024 when he reportedly lost $20 million playing poker in Montenegro. He is, according to Farage, 'like a son to me'. The PM has tasked him with handling the biggest bet of his political life.

Support for Scottish independence has rocketed in recent months as many north of the border grew infuriated by the right-wing agenda of the government in Westminster. As Stephen Flynn had said immediately on Farage's election as Prime Minister, the SNP had a growing mandate among the public for their demand to hold another referendum on the independence question. They argued it had been more than 15 years since the vote in 2014, which at the time people had said was intended to settle the question 'for a generation'. Now many felt that generation had passed and every week the SNP's leader of the Commons had stood up in PMQs in front of his 45 MPs and demanded Farage give him a vote.

In the present crisis, the support of SNP MPs in return for a commitment to hold an independence referendum would get Farage's budget over the line in the Commons and might allow space for Reform to regroup. He was only 27 votes short: First Minister John Swinney could save his administration. There was still a chance. There would be additional benefits for Farage too: with Scotland independent, Reform would have a greater chance at winning the next election if they are able to consolidate their power in England and Wales. Cottrell is adept at keeping a low profile: he's often seen at Reform events in dark sunglasses, performing an obscure role for his leader. One colleague said of working for the party in 2025: 'There is one rule: don't ask what George does'. Cottrell now has his orders and begins to make calls.

Meanwhile, a giant blimp in the shape of a limpet – which sections of the media had dubbed the 'blimpet' – with Nigel Farage's face on it floats over Trafalgar Square as the largest protest since the Iraq War takes place, with well over a million people making their way down Whitehall and past Downing Street in protest at Farage's actions. Later in the afternoon, violent scuffles break out and police on horseback have to use tear gas to disperse protesters. Hundreds are arrested on terrorism charges. The Home

Secretary James Orr attempts to convene a COBR meeting to address concerns from the police and security services about a threat to widespread public disorder, but Farage has barricaded himself into the upstairs flat at No 11.

Wednesday, 4 December 2030, 10 a.m.

The following day, John Swinney stands in front of the national media in a hastily arranged press conference at Bute House: 'Yesterday, a member of the prime minister's team made contact with an SNP colleague of mine and offered Scotland a referendum on its independence in exchange for us propping up his pathetic government and his disgraceful attempt to stay in Downing Street. The Scottish National Party will never do squalid backroom deals to shore up far-right administrations south of the border.'

In fact, Swinney had spent a sleepless night debating with his inner team whether to accept the proposal. He believes such is the strength of opinion in favour of independence, the Scottish public will vote for it regardless of its genesis. 'We would finally be free,' one of his passionate young advisors declared. Swinney agreed and drafted a letter to his party explaining that he was taking the 'difficult decision to back Reform tomorrow' in exchange for Scotland's freedom. The First Minister has secured assurances from George Cottrell that in return for voting with the government, he will receive a legally binding agreement for a referendum in which the SNP are allowed to set the terms.

But that morning, at the last minute, he had been pulled on to a video call with a group of eight SNP MPs who had got wind of the potential agreement: they told him directly that if he made a deal with the devil, they could not count on his support and it would split the Party.

The revelation that Farage had attempted to break up the union in order to save his premiership sends Reform MPs into meltdown and the Downing Street press room calls every single journalist in their contact books to deny Swinney's statement. Disbelieving that their dear leader would countenance such a tactic, many Reform MPs still loyal to the PM dismiss the statement as fake news and another example of the Opposition's mendacity.

10:30 a.m.

Lord Pannick KC, the highly regarded advocate who acted for Gina Miller when the Supreme Court ruled Boris Johnson's attempt to prorogue parliament was unlawful in 2019, writes a letter to *The Times* saying that he intends to pursue legal action against the PM, arguing that the will of the Commons in demanding Farage resigns be made legally enforceable. He cites the PM's 'flagrant abuse of parliamentary sovereignty'. A screenshot of the letter goes viral along with a link to the crowdfunder for the case, and barristers on Bluesky spend the afternoon trying to find ways in on the wording of a claim to defeat Farage in the courts.

11 a.m.

Meanwhile, the House of Commons is in disarray: the Speaker, a Farage loyalist, refuses to take her seat in the chamber and the Chaplain refuses to say prayers before debates. The Commons' Serjeant at Arms has to break up another fight in the Commons between Faragists and rebels, and a Lib Dem MP is floored after getting caught in the middle of it all. Videos on social media show MPs running after each other through the long corridors of the Palace, with SNP and Plaid MPs leading the charge. The deputy Speaker suspends all sittings of the House in an attempt to bring some order.

A helicopter tracks the Speaker's car as she makes her way to the Palace. The Speaker has both the right and responsibility to act in the scenario of a prime minister refusing to leave Downing Street. She should be heading to the Palace to discuss how the King may pressurise Farage into stepping down. In 1642, the Speaker, William Lenthall, resisted pressure from the monarch, Charles I, when his men tried to enter the Commons and arrest five members. This time, the Speaker should be acting to uphold the rights of Parliament to deal with a crisis precipitated by the democratically elected leader of Reform UK. But in this scenario, Farage got rid of her predecessor during the Great Repeal Bill debates, and managed to install a client into the post. This is where her deputy, sitting beside her in the car, will become important – behind the scenes, can she manage to bring the right individuals together to extricate the limpet?

As the car rounds St James's Park, Beth Rigby is telling viewers: 'The question that the whole country wants to know the answer to is whether the King will invoke his personal prerogative and dissolve Parliament. This immediately triggers another general election, but it is a move fraught with risk. While it might seem very tempting to remove the prime minister and cut the Gordian Knot, it will surely damage the King personally and raise questions about the legitimacy of the monarchy itself. On the other hand, many would praise the King for acting where Parliament has been unable to and argue that Farage has already assaulted constitutional convention in such a way that it invalidates any claim he makes against the rights of the King.'

Britain lies in an unprecedented constitutional crisis and its only backstop is an 81-year-old bedridden monarch with no democratic legitimacy. In normal circumstances during a change of government, the shorthand of Palace officials is for the 'cameras to be concentrated at the Whitehall end of The Mall, not ours'. This has suddenly become impossible. In this scenario, the role of the private secretary to the monarch Sir Clive Alderton becomes even more important: it is he who has been arranging for Opposition party leaders to come to the Palace to discuss with the King whether they have enough support to form a government in the gaze of the world's media. Constitutionally, it is thoroughly proper for a monarch to consult other party leaders on whether they could command the confidence of the Commons. His next job is to draft Charles's address to the nation.

6 p.m.

'I'm speaking to you at a time when it appears the precious principles of constitutional government which lie at the heart of our nation are under question. I would like to stress to leaders of all parties that in a democracy like ours, we have much to lose and those traditions which our forefathers fought for are a deeply special inheritance. As my mother did when she was alive, I solemnly promise to uphold these constitutional principles for as long as I am able.'

The BBC, under the control of Paul Dacre and his push to 'restore impartiality', interviews dozens of Reform outriders across its suite of radio and television channels, who call for an inquiry into the abolition of the monarchy following the King's statement. It broadcasts the speech in full live, but buries it online and it doesn't appear on iPlayer. The King's personal private secretary believes that the statement was a risk worth taking to put further pressure on Farage without formally demanding his resignation or dissolving Parliament. However, it is only a risk worth taking because the King still enjoys strong support across the country, but also across key institutions which become politically important at a time of constitutional crisis. As Commander-in-Chief of the Armed Forces, the King commands more loyalty from those exercising violence on the state's behalf than the prime minister does. In contrast to America, one benefit of the parlous current state of the British Army is that it might struggle to be put to much use in a situation where a prime minister co-opts military force for their own political ends.

6.15 p.m.

After his speech ends, the King retires to his private apartments with Queen Camilla. But Sir Clive Alderton is concerned: there had been briefings in the press that Farage was going to attempt one final, mad ploy to remain as Prime Minister. The *Telegraph* had received a leak from a Downing Street source that Farage was intent on ordering the King to prorogue Parliament. Alderton could not allow this to happen.

As comical as it sounds, the Palace had been forced to deal with this sort of behaviour just eight years previously, when Boris Johnson wished to request the Queen to dissolve Parliament and call an election following the resignations of his Cabinet in July 2022. The Palace and senior civil servants developed a 'wheeze' in which they would tell Johnson the Queen was too ill to get to the phone and accept his request. In our scenario, with the role of the cabinet secretary and the PPS politicised, it is more difficult for Alderton to cooperate with officials in Downing Street, but he convenes a meeting with trusted courtiers to ensure Farage is unable to make the request. But there are no guarantees and the Johnson precedent demonstrates the weak foundations of the 'good chaps' approach to constitutional affairs.

Thursday, 5 December 2030, 8.45 a.m.

A snap poll shows that in a matter of days, the public has turned against the prime minister and is blaming him for the chaos in Westminster. A vox pop with a man riding a mobility scooter down a high street in Cardiff sums up the national mood: 'No one likes a sore loser, do they? If they don't want Scotland then maybe we should go our own way too.'

At 9 a.m., the King is hosting the Speaker and the leaders of all the Opposition parties, as well as a representative from the former-Reform dissenters. The Reform-appointed Speaker disrupts the meeting by blaming the SNP for the disruption by not accepting Farage's deal, and the discussion ends in chaos. She retreats back to Parliament, but her deputy stays behind. She goes to the King and implores him to call back the leaders of the main parties, and they all reconvene in the Audience Room to hear her idea. If Parliament were to pass a 'humble address' to the monarch on the floor that day, and it was delivered to the Palace, the King would be able to demand the resignation of Farage with a fig-leaf of democratic legitimacy. Charles is in bed, barely able to respond. Sir Clive Alderton kneels by his side and whispers in his ear; the King nods his approval.

A humble address is a formal message from Parliament to the King. It can be used to request the government publish official papers: MPs passed a humble address introduced by Keir Starmer in 2017 to force the publication of details relating to the impact of Brexit. But they are a rarely used mechanism: Starmer's motion was the first time a humble address had been used since the nineteenth century. As they are addressed to the monarch, it can also function as a way for Parliament to make a claim on the King – in this case, to ask the King to use his prerogative and sack Farage. The Deputy Speaker and the Opposition party leaders ride back separately to the Commons, where the motion is tabled. The Speaker finds it impossible to refuse the request for a vote from all the opposition party leaders. The humble address to the King passes the House and begins being prepared by the clerks of the House. Meanwhile, the monarch issues a statement saying that he has received the Address and is acting upon it and asking for the prime minister's resignation. Farage is set to be legally sacked as Prime Minister, and it should be the end of his life in politics.

But what if the prime minister still won't go?

12 p.m.

Alderton picks up the phone to the head of the Metropolitan Police. If Farage still doesn't vacate No 10 after the King has asked for his resignation then the military and the police begin to come into play. In a world where politicians have lost control, the individuals the state employs to inflict violence are the final cards the establishment has to play. The monarch's private secretary can call anyone they want and has access to each important player. Alderton picks up the phone to the commissioner, who is sat in his office just over the road from Downing Street in New Scotland Yard. Alderton is calling to remind him that by choosing to become a squatter following the King's request, Farage is breaking the law.

12.10 p.m.

The commissioner must then make a judgement call as to whether he can – and should – arrest an intruder in Downing Street. The status of the Reform Cabinet is now relevant: with ministers resigning on X every 10 minutes, the commissioner can see it would be difficult for the prime minister to call on any significant political players to defend him or attack the police. The commissioner finds himself in an unprecedented situation: how does he make sure he comes out of this unscathed? Does he want to be the person who tried to get rid of Farage and failed, only to find himself at the mercy of a vengeful authoritarian prime minister? On the other hand, if he doesn't do anything, and they get rid of him anyway, will he be remembered as the policeman who blinked in the moment of Britain's greatest constitutional peril?

12.20 p.m.

The commissioner picks up the phone. The head of police security in Downing Street answers. He has been waiting in the guard tower by the gates of Downing Street for orders. The commissioner asks his subordinate to 'have a word' with Farage's wife, Laure. Unlike the commissioner, the head of police security knows Laure and all Farage's staff by name. The commissioner says he wants everything to be done to resolve the crisis without using force. The head of security leaves his gun in the booth and heads into Downing Street.

He knocks on the door of the No 11 flat and asks to come in, then sits down beside Laure: 'We've had word from further up. We don't want to do this, Laure, but we don't have a choice. If the prime minister doesn't leave within the next half an hour then I have orders to arrest him. We don't want a scene, which is why I'm coming to you first. The last thing anyone wants is for your husband to be led out in handcuffs in front of the cameras.'

Laure knocks on the door of the den. Farage unlocks it, checks who it is, and lets her in. A waft of cigarette smoke escapes from the room as she enters. She sits down beside him, holds his hand and presents him with the statement from the King and the poll showing the country has turned against him. Tice, Yusuf, Braverman and Jenrick have all gone, but Farage refuses to believe this until Laure shows him their letters of resignation. She shows him a video of Jukes pushing through a scrum of cameras at Heathrow airport as he boarded a flight out of the country.

When she closed the door, the last loyal advisors stood waiting in the Cabinet Room. There was a look of relief on her face. 'Give him a minute, but he'll come,' she said. It was over. The head of police security made sure to send an officer to help with his bags and see Farage off as he drove his own car out of the back of Downing Street. He had his handcuffs with him, just in case.

It takes a year for the next prime minister to get the smell of cigarettes and the red wine stains out of the carpet in the den of Downing Street. Other things stick around too: the collective noun for a disgraced group of former Reform MPs trying to make their way on GB News is 'limpets', the mollusc becoming an unlikely permanent symbol of the economic, political and constitutional wreckage Farage and his gang caused.

Although Britain had long ago stopped finding them funny, the limpets still managed to have a laugh. For some, being briefly a member of parliament was the most exciting time of their lives, and like old veterans from the war, they sometimes got together to remember.

After power, many of the old party divisions had evaporated, and there was a raucous atmosphere on one such occasion, a year after Farage's downfall, at a private room at the back of The Rifleman pub in Kent. Lee Anderson brandished a gavel as he compered an auction to raise money to cover the party's debts, and to help towards Farage's legal fees. They wanted 5 Hertford Street, but they had to be sensible with what money they had left.

For collectors of political memorabilia, the sale was a goldmine. Many turned up predicting the items would only increase in value, as Britain's curious Reform convulsion drifted into legend. Anderson offered his T-shirt cannon aloft to the audience, with some stubbing out their cigarettes outside to head back indoors for the bidding. Other lots included James Orr's signed copy of Erskine May, the bucket used to chuck flood water at Farage from the pub during his visit to Bristol, one of Cummings' beanies, and someone had even managed to track down the 'blimpet' flown over Trafalgar Square in the dying days of the government. Each lot was sold by the former politician associated with it: David Wimble, the former water and food security minister, was devastated to see his Reform-branded taxi cab sell for only £500 to a scrap metal dealer, who had wandered into the room from the bar. The MPs and donors collapsed into laughter as Wimble refused to agree the sale with the man, who challenged him to a fight outside.

Despite their high spirits, not far from any of their minds was the prospect of being dragged in front of the public inquiry into the constitutional stand-off between Farage and the country. Least of all the former PM, who had resorted to filming clips from the video sharing app Cameo once more to pay the astronomical fees relating to the inquiry and the other myriad legal threats he was facing. His income from American broadcasters had dried up, and he even briefly considered running for parliament again in Clacton, but his agent said the risk that Chabuddy G would win was too grave. Notably absent from the pub is Richard Tice, whose wife Isabel Oakeshott publishes a tell-all bestseller on the chaos of Farage's Downing Street. The inquiry would be sure to ask plenty of questions about its contents. The former PM makes sure to shake the hand of as many donors as possible at The Rifleman – unbelievably, there were still a handful who hadn't moved back to the Tories – and they each cursed the name of the former DG of the BBC who had been chosen as the inquiry's Chair.

An important question it would consider was whether to recommend that Britain adopts a formal, written constitution. There had been many attempts at this in the past, but as political leaders surveyed the damage, and with the tacit support of the King, the idea became an issue at the next election. Even Tommy Robinson, who is running in Luton as an independent, is in favour of it to protect free speech. He is angling for an invitation to a summit at Kew, where potential articles will be discussed. But the anti-Farage political coalition had vanished after the limpet had left Downing Street, and many Opposition MPs said the cost of the inquiry, estimated to be over £200 million, was a waste: its proposals would never be implemented and its findings ignored, they said, while others argued it was reasonable given that the Reform hit to the economy was north of £200 billion. It seemed possible that Britain, divided and squabbling, would learn nothing from the events of 2030.

But there were many who were determined for that not to be the case. One was the former deputy speaker, who had been chosen by MPs for promotion, who strengthened procedure and the rights of parliamentarians. One of the debates she gave time for was proposals for constitutional rights to protect nature, something the arch opportunist and former occupant of No 10 might well have supported, had he wanted to win votes in his native county of Kent. The formerly 'gin-clear' riverbeds had become murky and polluted after an accident at the fracking plant Farage had announced. Frack fluid, containing heavy metals and salts, gushed for weeks unnoticed into the clear water until it was too late. The well was abandoned not long after: it became a noted architectural quirk, an industrial folly symbolising Britain's 'limpet' moment. But nearby, far from the media's gaze and Westminster, a local group forms to do something about it.

They make a deal with the local farmer to divert the run-off pipe, plant new trees, and create offshoots to provide a place for fish to thrive. They are delighted when the green shoots of reeds begin to re-emerge from the previously barren banks, and resolve to write to the organisers of the Kew summit in support of the article for nature.

In 2026, to many a Reform government feels like a spectre on the edge of the horizon, an oil slick whose poisonous effects have not yet lapped on to the shore. But with just three years until the next general election, the arrival of that new, dark reality is fast approaching. Those who wish to avert the disaster still have time to remember a different future is possible, and act.

Acknowledgements

Thank you to everyone at Bloomsbury, especially Tomasz Hoskins, Allie Collins, Jessica Gray, Sarah Head and James Watson, as well as my agent at Peters Fraser and Dunlop, Elizabeth Sheinkman. I would also like to thank everyone I spoke to for the book, and to my first readers, Jamie Sandall and Bethany Appleton.

But there are three people in particular to which I owe a great debt. Thank you to my mother, for kindness and belief; to Octavia Stocker, for your dedication and judgement; and to Eleanor, for your wisdom and love.